Instructional Designer Competencies

The Standards, Fourth Edition

A Volume in
Ibstpi Book Series

ibstpi INTERNATIONAL BOARD OF STANDARDS FOR
TRAINING, PERFORMANCE AND INSTRUCTION

Ibstpi Book Series

Instructor Competencies:
Standards for Face-to-Face, Online, and Blended Settings (2004)
by James D. Klein, J. Michael Spector,
Barbara Grabowski, and Ileana de la Teja

Online Learner Competencies: Knowledge, Skills, and Attitudes for
Successful Learning in Online Settings (2013)
by Michael Beaudoin, Insung Jung,
Katsuaki Suzuki, Gila Kurtz, and Barbara Grabowski

Instructional Designer Competencies:
The Standards, Fourth Edition (2013)
by Tiffany A. Koszalka, Darlene F. Russ-Eft,
Robert Reiser, and Fernando A. Senior

DEDICATIONS

This book is dedicated to all previous and current ibstpi® board directors for their insights, challenges, and drive to enhance the global practices of those in the training, performance, and instruction professions.

We would like to acknowledge the many persons who have participated in the development and validation of these newly revised ID Competencies. We especially thank the following previous directors for their guidance and feedback—Rita Richey, Marguerite Foxon, Timothy Spannaus, J. Michael Spector, and Barbara L. Grabowski.

These competencies have also been influenced by many persons who provided input and reactions—both formally and informally—throughout the redevelopment and validation process. This includes alumni from Instructional Design programs at Florida State and Syracuse Universities, practicing instructional designers from business, government and military, private consulting, and other contexts, academics in higher education and K-12, those studying to be instructional designers, members of several professional associations including Association of Educational and Communication Technology (AECT); International Society of Performance Improvement (ISPI), Academy of Human Resources Development (AHRD), American Society for Training and Development (ASTD) with their global affiliates, and countless others. We thank you all.

Finally, we offer this volume in a special tribute to David H Jonassen. His work was not focused on instructional designer competencies, however he had a profound influence on practitioners, researchers, and scholars in our field, worldwide—how we think, how we seek understanding, how we design, how we practice, and how we develop as a community of professionals.

The ibstpi Board of Directors

Instructional Designer Competencies

The Standards, Fourth Edition

by

Tiffany A. Koszalka
Syracuse University

Darlene F. Russ-Eft
Oregon State University

Robert Reiser
Florida State University

with

Fernando A. Senior Canela,

Barbara L. Grabowski,

and

Clinton J. Wallington

Information Age Publishing, Inc.
Charlotte, North Carolina • www.infoagepub.com

Library of Congress Cataloging-in-Publication Data

CIP data for this book can be found on the Library of Congress website http://
www.loc.gov/index.html

ISBNs: Paperback: 978-1-62396-403-0
         Hardcover: 978-1-62396-404-7
         eBook: 978-1-62396-405-4

CONTENTS

FOREWORD

IBSTPI—THE DEVELOPMENT ORGANIZATION

What beliefs motivate a group of professionals to create a standards development organization? Perhaps, in 1977, for the joint group of professional practitioners, researchers and scientists from The Association for Educational Communications and Technology (AECT) and the National Society for Performance Improvement (NSPI—now ISPI), it was a fervent belief that performance could be improved by well designed, high quality instruction, training, and learning interventions. Evolving from this joint initiative, The International Board of Standards for Training, Performance and Instruction (ibstpi)[1] was incorporated in 1984 as an unbiased, independent group, and continues to this day. The board, then and now, broadly represents those audiences in which performance counts—that is, in universities, schools, government, business, industry, medicine, adult education, consulting, etc. across international contexts. Fifteen international, elected directors are bound together by a common mission: to develop, validate and promote implementation of international standards to advance training, instruction, learning and performance improvement.

WHY ADOPT IBSTPI COMPETENCIES?

Other versions of performance standards and processes for developing them have been created by other organizations. What distinguishes the ibstpi competencies from others is the rigorous development process that the ibstpi research and development team follows. The process requires multidimensional input from research advancements, accepted, current

Instructional Designer Competencies: The Standards, Fourth Edition, pp. ix–xii
Copyright © 2013 by Information Age Publishing
All rights of reproduction in any form reserved.

standards of practice, ethics, values, culture, and visions of the future. The ibstpi research team determinedly sifts through this input, and from this input drafts the initial set of competencies and performance statements. This draft set is then validated by an international body of professionals who fill various versions of the job, representing varying levels of experience and expertise, as well as academics and those who oversee or provide input to the job. The results are meticulously developed and validated international standards of performance for a specific job skill. See Chapters 1 and 5 for more detail on this process and the results that lend support for the credence, criticality, and comprehensiveness of the current set of Instructional Designer Competencies.

THE CURRENT STATE

When one addresses the "sense" of instructional design, that is, the creation of learning interventions to promote performance improvement, and how it is changed over the years, one is struck with the realization that it is competence in the process of thinking at higher levels that influences the ability of an instructional designer be effective at his or her job. The ability to think analytically, evaluate, and synthesize multidimensional data from multiple sources to solve a learning problem is as equally important today as it was hundreds of years ago, and as more recently articulated in the previous sets of ID competencies (1993, 2000). These fundamental thinking skills must be executed masterfully in systemic (and yes, systematic) thinking. Regardless of how small or how formal, learning happens within a system of people, objects, situation, and actions.

The competency development team has captured and articulated these fundamental thinking skills in the current 5 domains, 23 competencies, and 105 performance statements. To be a competent instructional designer still requires the ability to plan, analyze the situation, create and develop designs for learning interventions, implement and evaluate those designs to determine their level of effectiveness regardless of philosophical orientation. These specific proficiencies are demonstrated through 14 competencies statements distributed in three of the five domains: planning and analysis, design and development, evaluation and implementation. Also, ibstpi continues to adhere to foundational professional competencies that underlie any field. Those competencies are represented in the professional foundations domain. The ibstpi research and development team has added an important domain that recognizes the expanded role of an instructional designer, that of managerial competencies articulated in the Management domain.

NOTABLES

Three other very important contributions of this book add value to this set of competencies. They include (1) a clear articulation of current roles and responsibilities of instructional designers in the evolving field of learning, (2) the addition of a third classification of competence level, managerial, and (3) a delineation of competencies for ID specializations.

The evolving complexity of roles, responsibilities and design activities. The discussion in Chapter 1 skillfully captures the impact of changes to the field of instructional design caused by an expanded work environment, the span of complexity to learning problems instructional designers face, and the span of technological sophistication of learners within an expanded learning environment that includes anytime, anyplace, many learning tools. Through this discussion, the reader will discern how these changes transform a competency statement that is seemingly the same as was written in 2004. The words may be the same, but the practice and implementation is vastly different because of the current state of the learning system. Look for these repeated issues having an immense impact on competency demonstration:

Complexity of the ID Roles and Responsibilities

- expanded instructional design job role in a vastly different job setting, including teams and distributed expertise, in distributed locales;
- vastly expanded, more technologically sophisticated and efficient design tools;
- an evolving understanding of learning, with required expertise in the design sciences impacting potential design approaches;
- changed economic expectations of clients for faster development of cost effective course offerings;
- complex problems.

Complexity of Design Activities

- a span of technologically sophisticated and socially connected learners with higher expectations from their learning materials and activities;
- broad cultural diversity;
- expanded and more sophisticated learning tools;

- expanded opportunities for networked activities that now includes anytime, anyplace, many tools, and social networking;
- expanded literacy requirements.

Levels of competence. Including two levels of competence, essential (for novice instructional designers) and advanced (for experienced instructional designers) is a signature characteristic of previous versions of the ID competencies. The authors, in recognition of the expanded roles and responsibilities of some instructional designers, added a third level of competence to this set to emphasize the importance of managerial skills to instructional design function managers.

Specializations. The authors recognize a growing trend of some employers expecting specialized instructional design skills in a subset rather than the entire set of instructional design competencies. This specialization expectation has evolved because of the complexity of learning problems and situations, learning or performance orientation of the organization, or even distribution of learners. To address this trend, the authors specify four specializations, ID specialists, analysis/evaluator, id manager, and e-learning/instructional technology specialist. Primary and supporting competencies and performance statements have been selected and matched to each of these specialties.

CONCLUSION

Indeed, these internationally validated instructional designer competencies, along with the accompanying discussion, contributes to the fulfillment of ibstpi's mission to advance training, instruction, learning and performance improvement. As an elected board of directors with broad international representation, ibstpi continues to set the standards.

Barbara L. Grabowski, PhD
ibstpi Fellow
Former ibstpi President (2004-2010)
Professor Emerita of Instructional Systems, The Pennsylvania State University

NOTE

1.   See http://www.ibstpi.org for more information.

PREFACE

One third of a century. Sounds like a long time. And it is. But that is about how long the ibstpi instructional design standards have been around. Not that they are the same as they were 34 years ago. Many are fundamentally the same. Yet in many ways they have changed quite a bit.

One Example (of Many)

At the founding of the standards, no one anticipated a handheld computing device and social media. In fact, the first *ibstpi* committee meeting was held the same year (1977) that the Apple II was introduced.[1] This edition reflects (generically) a radically changed population of learners.

Another Example

Developed predominantly by AECT people when ISPI was still NSPI[2], the first edition of the standards pretty much overlooked performance interventions. This edition incorporates them as an integral part of the competencies.

There were only 16 instructional design competencies in the first edition (1986).

That expanded to 24 in the second edition and contracts to 22 in this edition—while losing two of the first 16 (*interacting effectively with people* and *promoting the use of instructional design*). The net result is major expansion in the areas of design and professionalism. Another big change from the first edition is grouping the competencies into four

Instructional Designer Competencies: The Standards, Fourth Edition, pp. xiii–xvi
Copyright © 2013 by Information Age Publishing

core areas and the differentiation between essential and advanced competencies.

The intent herein is not to offer any sort of detailed history of nor a rationale for the competencies.[3] Instead, it is more intended to illustrate and emphasize that the competencies are alive and vibrant, And (thanks to some extremely hardworking practitioners), the standards both keep up with—as well as anticipate—the needs of and trends in instructional design.[4]

What is the Same and What is Different?

As mentioned there are two fewer competencies in this edition, but there are five competency areas rather than four. "Implementation and Management" (from 2000) has become "Evaluation and Implementation" and "Management." In addition there is a new competency classification, "managerial" to complement "essential" and "advanced."

Rather than a detailed comparison of the last set of competencies and the new ones, let me touch only on the highlights.

The five competencies in the "professional foundations" cluster remain much the same, albeit updated.

The seven competences in the previous edition's "planning and analysis" cluster have been reduced to four. The competencies have not been lost; for the most part they have been merged into the current competencies.

The "design and development cluster" still has seven competencies, but with increased emphasis on interventions (whether instructional or not) rather than only *instruction*.

The new "evaluation and implementation" cluster and the new "management" cluster each have three competencies based mostly on the previous "implementation and management" cluster. The new "evaluation and implementation" cluster recognizes the growth of noninstructional interventions as a key part of performance improvement. The new "managerial" cluster reflects the growing influence of instructional design as part of management decision making. These two new clusters merit at least a cursory study for those with ties to the management of performance improvement of a unit.

Why?

Finally, Chapter 1 of this edition should be required reading for the underlying rationale behind the revised competencies.

Chapter 1 gives the logic behind those changes, and supports that rationale with research.[5] The research summary has, and will continue to, put instructional design beyond a set of eclectic, ad hoc practices.

Moreover, the chapter explains how the competency model was developed as well as 10 basic assumptions that underlie the model and the competencies.

In closing, I offer my personal congratulations to the devoted people who worked to make this edition possible. I am honestly staggered at what dedicated people have done to grow a now naive-seeming set of 16 basic competencies 34 years old. I salute you and all those that have worked so hard on the previous edition.

Now that you are feeling good, here is the catch. Do not relax too much. It took from 1977 to 1986 to get the first edition (small as it was) out. Fourteen years elapsed between the first and the second edition. From that edition until now, only 11 years have passed. Take a very short break and start planning the next edition. If the pattern holds, there is only about 8 years to get it done.

More seriously, my most sincere congratulations and thanks to all those people—especially those working on this edition—who have turned a germ of an idea into a significant and potent reality.

Clint J. Wallington; 2012
Professor—Rochester Institute of Technology, NY
Member of the initial taskforce on ID certification begun in 1979

NOTES

1. I take part of the blame for the acronym "ibstpi." I was working at a national association in Washington DC and very conscious of association marketing and branding. I pretty much insisted on having the concept of "international" in the association along with "training, performance, and instruction" to cover the content waterfront. I pushed hard for a more palatable acronym, but we never got around to making one. Hence, "ibstpi." Sorry.

2. ISPI figured out the value of the "international" branding and made the switch from national to international in its name. Coincidentally, I was on its board when that happened.

3. Rob Foshay's rationale in the preface to the previous edition is excellent and pretty much timeless. It is well worth reading if instructional design is your primary occupation.

4. You could make the case that "instructional" may not be the appropriate term any more, but there's something to be said for tradition—and that is a decision for the next committee.

5.   I suppose this is an example of instructional design competency #2, that is, "Apply research and theory to the discipline of instructional design." The committee practices what it preaches. Bravo!

CHAPTER 1

INSTRUCTIONAL DESIGNER COMPETENCE

INSTRUCTIONAL DESIGNER COMPETENCE: AN INTRODUCTION

In 1986, the International Board of Standards for Training, Performance and Instruction (ibstpi) published the first edition of *Instructional Design Competencies: The Standards*. This was a culmination of work that began by a taskforce of recognized instructional design experts in 1978. Initial drafts of the designer competency list evolved between 1979-1983 (Task Force on ID Certification, 1981). In retrospect, this work occurred in the infancy (or at least the toddler years) of the practice community now commonly referred to as *instructional designers*. And, although there were earlier descriptions of instructional designer competencies (Wallington, 1981) and other suggested sets, none have been as well researched, validated, and accepted globally as the instructional designer standards as ibstpi's.

In 2000, ibstpi published it second generation of the competencies. These standards were a greatly expanded view of the work of the instructional designer that reflected the complexities of then, current practices and technologies, theoretical advancements, and the social tenor of the times. Nonetheless, it was a view that was still rooted in the traditional notion of design competence. In fact, the instructional design discipline has contributed to improving learning in organization and educational environments for decades. The profession itself, informed by many disciplines, has now migrated toward the challenges of designing instructional and learning solutions in the 21st century. This includes effectively

Instructional Designer Competencies: The Standards, Fourth Edition, pp. 1–21
Copyright © 2013 by Information Age Publishing
All rights of reproduction in any form reserved.

incorporating the many unprecedented emerging technologies. Constant in the growth of this community of practice is the continual use of fundamentals of the design sciences to create solutions.

ibstpi is now proud to release its most current 2012 version of the instructional designer (ID) competencies. This set was developed through a rigorous research process including reviews of the current literature, engagement of experts, and an international validation by over 1,000 instructional design practitioners and scholars from different work environments, cultures, and educational backgrounds. Rooted in a traditional notion of design competence this set further expands the depth of the competencies and their performance statements and more thoroughly attends to the explosion of technologies that have entered into the designer's and educator's communities of practices.

This chapter lays the foundation for the updated ibstpi ID competencies. It briefly summarizes the changes in instructional design practice since 2000, examines the ibstpi competency development model and the assumptions central to the development, and the revisions made to this updated set of competencies.

INSTRUCTIONAL DESIGN: YESTERDAY AND TODAY

The foundations for the practices of ID are made up of an eclectic collection of theories and practices that have multiple origins. Theoretically, instructional design is rooted in theories of general systems, learning, communications, and instruction (Richey, 1986). The field's 20th century practice origins were in the military training demands of World War II (Dick, 1987; Seels, 1989). Gustafson and Branch (1997) credit the Barson model used at Michigan State University between 1961 and 1965 as being one of the first ID models. However, it was not until the 1970s that the term "instructional design" was commonly used. Instead, most "designers" called themselves educational psychologists, media specialists, or training specialists (Dick, 1987). Dick and Carey's now classic book, *The Systematic Design of Instruction*, was not published until 1978—only one year before the first draft of the original ibstpi ID competencies that were ultimately published in 1986.

For the most part, the early ID models had a product orientation. The model was directed more toward the design and development of a product, but not the implementation and maintenance of that product in a given environment. With the exception of the work of Leonard Silvern (1971), these design projects occurred either in a higher education setting or were focused on producing instruction for elementary and secondary schools.

In the 1980s the preponderance of instructional design practices had occurred within the private sector, primarily in business and industrial settings. This coincides with a steady growth of employee training as an integral part of most organizations. In the United States alone, the training industry was a $62.5 billion endeavor in 1999, up from the 1990 estimates of $45.4 billion, and 1985 estimates of $30 billion as reported by the American Society of Training and Development (ASTD) (Industry Report, 1990, 1999). In 2009 training industry boasted over $125 billion investment in employee training (ASTD, 2011). Remarkably, these data are only partially descriptive, since they reflect only direct costs of formal training in organizations with 100 or more employees. Informal, on-the-job training and a plethora of workshops, online instruction, social media instructional activities, and other endeavors dedicated to increasing human performance are not included. Training in smaller firms throughout the United States and international expenditures are not included. Moreover, such growth was not unique to the United States; rather the growth was duplicated to a greater extent worldwide. This growth reflected an emphasis on producing a more knowledgeable workforce. It also increasingly focused on improving employee on-the-job performance and solving organizational human resources problems.

Correspondingly in the late 1990s and beyond, instructional design to many was not merely an organized approach to product or course development, it was a generic process for analyzing human performance problems and determining appropriate instructional and noninstructional solutions to such problems. In addition, designers and training managers were often tasked with predicting future problems, likely organizational changes, and new ways to prepare employees for these new situations (Pieters, 1997). These changes in orientation were a dominate factor that served as the foundation of the 2000 edition of ibstpi instructional design competencies.

CHANGES THAT LED TO THIS CURRENT VERSION

The settings for, and conditions under which, ID work has continually changed over the years provides a backdrop for the emergence of new complex practices. Instructional designers have moved from working as individuals to working in interdisciplinary design teams, both in person and now more commonly through distributed communication channels. Designers are now often serving as consultants to internal or external clients who are looking for improvements in worker performance. Many designers are now working in academic environments creating instructional and learning solutions for younger and older students, spanning prekindergarten to senior citizen age ranges. Some environments are grant funded requiring adherence to educational and product development standards, while others are privately funded relying on the instructional designers' expertise to create successful instruction that meets the needs of the intended audience. Still others are working to convert analogue, face-to-face, and paper-based instruction to digital, online, virtual learning experiences.

Learners are also becoming more sophisticated users of technologies. This puts pressure on educational and training institutes to follow suit by integrating technologies successfully into their curriculum. This massive movement in integrating new technologies for teaching and learning processes potentially makes instruction more accessible and more easily completed at anytime, from any place. The global growth in mobile technologies (e.g., smartphones, tablets, i-technologies) for example, and efforts by higher education, K-12, and business organizations to take advantage of these portable devices and virtual spaces is only one example of the complex interaction between instructional design and emerging technologies (Koszalka & Ntloedibe-Kuswani, 2010) suggesting a need to update the ID competencies. Although the benefits of these new technologies can be great, the risks of poor design are distractions to, and hampering of, learning.

Changes in economics, expectations, and technologies are being matched by increased pressures to reduce the time required for design and development and increased expectations that instruction will have a positive impact on the educational mission and profits of an organization. The need for sound program evaluation competencies, for example, is growing rapidly to address this expectation (Russ-Eft, Bober, de la Teja, Foxon, & Koszalka, 2008). Changes in design tools and techniques, and correspondingly in expanded expectations for designer expertise are also at the foundation of the updates to the ID competencies.

The basic 1970s skills are now supplemented by new technology competencies (e.g., visual literacy, message design, screen design, interactivity design), business acumen (e.g., project management, cost analysis), and more sophisticated evaluation skills, for example. Designer career ladders continue to develop to match these new competencies. For example novice designers are most likely tasked with development activities, whereby needing strong development competencies (e.g., translating design specifications into instructional materials, working with production specialists to create technology resources). More advanced designers are likely tasked with designing more sophisticated instructional materials that take advantage of new technology tools (e.g., social media, web resources, learning management systems) without distracting from the learning process as well as specialty activities like conducting needs assessment and program evaluations. Managers of instructional design teams or functions are becoming more prevalent and expected to have all these competencies and a full set of project managements skills to facilitate teams in the design and development of instructional materials, often using multiple platforms for development and delivery.

Nowadays designers should be well versed in the design sciences (e.g., instruction, learning, message, visual, assessment), development sciences (e.g., production processes, project management, collaborative activities), and in the features of a variety of new media (e.g., video, hypermedia, social media) that lend themselves to facilitating different types of learning. We must be careful ***not*** to turn this into a movement that refocuses instructional designers into production or information technology specialists, rather it is critical to prepare instructional designers with the competencies that will help them align content, instructional and learning strategies, assessment, learner characteristics, and technologies when designing instruction to close identified performance gaps.

Designers must demonstrate their competencies through the use of systemic thinking practices (e.g., how instruction affects the individual and the organization, how materials and activities support learning) and choice of sound instructional design and development tools (e.g., knowledge, artifacts) to support their own productivity and maintain the high level of effectiveness and quality in designing and creating instructional solutions. They must be able to communicate effectively with multiple types of people and able to analyze an environment to determine knowledge and skills gaps that may be resolved by instructional and noninstructional solutions. They must understand how adults learn in the most complex environments. They must be able to successfully perform learning assessments, evaluation processes, and basic research. These types of competencies have been expressed and developed upon in earlier descriptions of competent instructional design professionals (Wallington, 1981).

As we have seen in this last decade emerging technologies (e.g., mobile, social-collaborative media, learning management systems, open sources code tools) that have drastically changed design tools and processes making technology development more efficient, less time consuming, and unfortunately many times (with unskilled instructional designers) not as effective. A programmer or web developer not well versed in instructional design often uses technology features for impact or visual appeal, ultimately and unwittingly distracting learners during instruction (Oliver, 1999; Underwood, Hoadly, Lee, DiGiano, & Renniger, 2005). Thus, design competencies are critical in the process of integrating technology resources or environments into instructional solutions.

In today's instructional design market, the field is no longer primarily an American endeavor. Instructional designers are working and being educated worldwide. As organizations expand beyond individual country boundaries, designers are addressing the issue of preparing and adapting instructional materials for different cultures, and to be offered in distributed platforms. This is done both by internationalizing the materials to make them more culture-free and by localizing products to make them more culturally depended (Richey & Morrison, 2000). Blended learning environments are being produced that facilitate in-person and virtually distributed synchronous and asynchronous learning events (Knox & Wilmott, 2008; Koszalka & Wu, 2010; Wu & Koszalka, 2011). Flexible informational, instructional, and learning resources are being produced that can be used for multiple purposes or adapted by learners to meet their own learning needs (Grabowski & Small, 1997; Wiley, 2002). It is through the creativity and instructional design competencies of instructional designers and their collaborative teams that such challenges can be successful and overcome the challenges presented by boundaries, distributed knowledge, and individual learner preferences in sophisticated technology-dependent environments.

The remainder of this chapter focuses on the conceptual and methodological frame underpinning the development of the ibstpi ID competencies. It begins with a brief history of competency modeling. Then, a brief examination of the context of the ibstpi competency development work and presentation of the definition of competency used in this book are presented. The reader will find a description of the generic ibstpi model used to develop the ID Competencies as well as the underlying assumptions serving in the development and interpretation of the model. The final section presents the ID Competencies model itself.

COMPETENCY AND THE IBSTPI COMPETENCY DEVELOPMENT MODEL

Competence and Competency

With the advent of performance-based educational techniques, competencies have served as the nucleus of program design and development efforts. This movement had various origins. One was the demand for clearly definable measures of program effectiveness in teacher education programs (Dick, Watson, & Kaufman, 1981). Competency-based education subscribed to the then innovative systems design techniques and elements of mastery learning (Young & Van Mondfrans, 1972). Competency-based education program design was widely used in both teacher education and K-12 education during the 1970s. These new programs coincided with the work of McClelland (1973) who outlined methods for the identification of competencies that provided nonbiased ways of predicting job performance. McCelland's competency approach was applied in organizational human resources functions of employee selection, career pathing, performance appraisals, and development. Today, competencies continue to be used in many of these same activities in the business environment.

Nonetheless, there are differing views of the nature of a competency and its relationship to professional competence. Parry (1998) cited the tendency for many to mistake competencies for personality traits or characteristics, or for styles and values. Lucia and Lepsinger (1999) see personal characteristics and aptitudes as foundational to skill and knowledge demonstration. It is generally agreed, however, that while competence is the state of being well qualified, competency statements are description of the critical ways in which such competence is demonstrated. Competencies are innately behavioral and positivistic in nature. Spencer and Spencer (1993) portrayed competency as with core or surface entities, with skills and knowledge being surface variables that are easier to develop than core characteristics such as attitudes.

McLagan (1997) identified six different approaches to competency definition. She noted that competencies have been viewed as job task, as results of work efforts, as outputs, as knowledge, skills, and attitudes, as qualities that describe superior performers, and finally as bundles of attributes.

ibstpi defines a competency as:

> a knowledge, skill, or attitude that enables one to effectively perform the activities of a given occupation or function to the standards expected in employment.

This orientation combines two of the McLagan competency definition models—that of job tasks and of an accumulation of knowledge, skills, and attitudes. The ibstpi competencies are statements of behavior—not personality traits or beliefs, but they do often reflect attitudes. ibstpi competencies are correlated with performance on a job and are typically measured against commonly accepted standards. Moreover, there is an implication that the ibstpi competencies can be developed through training. This is consistent with Parry's (1998) interpretation of the general nature of competency statements.

COMPETENCIES IN USE

Competencies have been used for many purposes in organizations. Lucia and Lepsinger (1999) described current manifestations of the functions initiated in the 1970s. These included interviewing prospective employees, hiring qualified persons, and facilitating effective performance appraisal and succession planning. Competencies were also critical to successful training since they clarify necessary job skills, focus training plans on missing competencies in the work forces, and provide a framework for coaching and feedback. Lucia and Lepsinger also cited the use of competency models as tools to determine those skills required to meet future needs of the organization. Competencies, such as the ibstpi ID competencies, can also serve a useful role in academe. They can be benchmarking tools for programs and a departure point for course planning and student assessment.

A BRIEF HISTORY OF COMPETENCY MODELING

Competency modeling refers to the process resulting in a cohesive description of human performance and the attributes of people required to perform effectively. That process yields a model, that is, an organized set of competencies and performance indicators. Some trace the first efforts of competency profiling to the early Romans in their attempts to describe the qualities of a *good Roman soldier* (Kierstead, 1998). However, given the various interpretations that the term *competency* has received, it would be difficult to find the exact roots of competency modeling, as we currently know it. Although Flanagan (1949, 1954), for example, never used the term *competency*, he pioneered techniques of collecting data on observable behaviors of employees, objectively evaluating performance, and determining requirements of an activity. It is commonly agreed, though, that competency modeling was initiated in the late 1960s and early 1970s with research done by David McCelland (1973) introducing competencies instead of academic aptitude or intelligence as an alternative way to measuring and predicting job performance, employee selection, and career development. More recently, the O*Net effort (http://www.onetcenter.org) resulted in defining a common dictionary for competencies.

More current research on competency modeling examines the relationships among the ever-increasing market pressures, leaner organizations, rapid economic changes, and career development (DeVos, DeHauw, & Van der Heijden, 2011) and workers' employability competencies (skills, knowledge, and attitudes) that are valued and that predict the potential for a successful career (Fugate & Kinicki, 2008; Fugate, Kinicki, & Ashforth, 2004; Van der Heijde & Van der Heijden, 2006). This work along with examinations of the competencies experts and novices (Eseryel, 2006; Gogus, Koszalka, & Spector, 2009; Koszalka & Epling, 2010; Spector, Dennen, & Koszalka, 2006) has helped define the critical nature of individual preparedness for their work, for example, development, monitoring, and improving of competence in light of constant change in the workplace.

THE IBSTPI COMPETENCY DEVELOPMENT MODEL

It was in the context of a competency-based movement assessing the effectiveness of teacher education programs (Dick, Watson, & Kaufman, 1981) and using systems design techniques and mastery learning (Dick, Carey, & Carey, 2005; Young & Van Mondfrans, 1972) that the ibstpi work on competency model development began to evolve.

The application of a competency-based approach can occur in many different settings, including academe/training, public and private sectors, and extending to nonprofit and professional organizations. In the light of this diversity of contexts and uses, it is not surprising that the nature of a competency and how it relates to professional competence itself can be viewed from different perspectives.

The nature of competence and competencies. The competency construct has been conceptualized in many ways (Catano, 1998; Le Boterf, 2001; Toolsema, 2003). Most of the definitions of competency focus on knowledge, skills and attitudes as main components of competencies (Lucia & Lepsinger, 1999; McLagan, 1997; Parry, 1998). A major divergent viewpoint exists concerning the personality traits, qualities, and values. According to Parry (1998), some mistake these personal attributes for the nature of competencies, instead of including them as foundational to skill and knowledge demonstration.

Similarly, the terms competence and competency are sometimes equated (Van Merriënboer, Van der Klink, & Hendriks, 2002). However some authors argue that there is a distinction between both concepts (Klein, 1996; Rowe, 1995; Woodruff, 1991). For Richey, Fields, and Foxon (2001), competence and competency are different but interrelated concepts: competence refers to the state of being well qualified, and a competency describes the critical ways in which competence is demonstrated.

The ibstpi generic competency development model. The set of competencies for a defined occupation or organizational role, such as the ibstpi instructional designer competencies, can be represented in a competency model. According to Marrelli (1998), a competency model refers to "the organization of identified competencies into a conceptual framework that enables the people in an organization to understand, talk about, and apply the competencies" (p. 10). Another definition specifies that a competency model includes the critical competencies that drive success for an occupation or a specific job, definitions for each competency, and a list of behavioral indicators for each competency that describe how the competency is demonstrated (HR Guide to the Internet, 2012). Thus, a competency model gives structure to a collection of competencies by organizing the knowledge, skills, and attitudes using a specific framework. Furthermore, it includes performance indicators describing how each competency is demonstrated in a job context.

To effectively build a competency model, ibstpi uses a generic competency development model that leverages input from several levels of analysis in order to define each competency. The model puts into perspective the link between the competencies, the job role, and how each competency is demonstrated (see Figure 1.1).

The first level (reading left to right), the definition of the *job role*, dictates the major orientation and scope of the competency model. Defining the *job role* tends to be a preliminary step to competency definition. For example, a role can be defined in a generic way or be customized or specific to a job context (Lucia & Lepsinger, 1999). The approach used in the ibstpi instructional designer competencies corresponds to a generalized view of the general instructional designer who works within a variety of organizational settings. According to their particular positions, different instructional designers may require only certain competencies articulated in the model. Indeed, it is highly unlikely that an instructional designer will need all of the competencies at any one time, but necessity for these competencies will emerge over the course of time, when engaging in different instructional projects, when in different settings, and when working with different requirements.

The *job roles* must be interpreted further to facilitate competency definition. At this second level of the development, specific *job behaviors* that are characteristic of the instructional designer are identified. For example, an important behavior for an instructional designer involves performing a needs assessment to identify instances and root causes of a performance problem. Standards of performance associated with the identified *job behaviors*, as well as the *professional values and ethics* prevailing in the field are also identified. Thus, in terms of conducting a needs assessment, the instructional designer should follow certain standards to ensure accuracy in the data collection and certain ethical guidelines to ensure confidentiality of the data. To complete this second level of analysis, it is essential to distinguish the *vision* that gives shape and direction to the instructional designer's role. "This vision may be the result of interpretations of current research and emerging trends, or it may be the result of societal or business pressures" (Foxon, Roberts, & Spannaus, 2003, p. 24).

A major issue at this stage of the analysis is balancing what appears as current practice with what ibstpi and our expert advisors believe the role

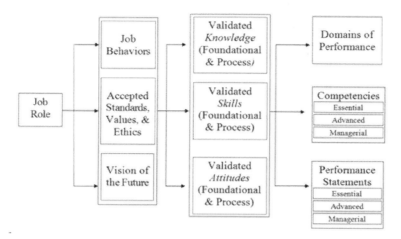

Figure 1.1. ibstpi competency model.

is or *should be*. It is the tension between the *what is* and the *what should be* and an analysis of trends and expectations of future visions of how the instructional designer role will develop over the next 5 to 10 years that influence the definition of the competencies. For example, ibstpi sees a trend toward more integration of emerging technologies into instructional products and environments. This trend has led to the inclusion of a performance statement on *acquiring new technology skills in instructional design practices*, for example.

The information gathered on behaviors, standards, ethics, values and vision of a job role guide the third level of analysis that results in the identification of **knowledge**, **skills**, and **attitudes** required by instructional designers to be competent in their work.

Finally, at a fourth level, this information is organized according to three components: *domains*, **competencies** and **performance statements**. In this case the model is further customized to include three levels (or classifications) of competencies for the instructional designer job, that of the **essential** (basic novice instructional designers should have these competencies), **advanced** (experienced instructional designers should posses these competencies and the essential competencies of the novice), and **managerial** (instructional design function managers should possess these competencies and those of the advanced and essential levels). This classification is replicated in the performance statements.

Structure of the ID Competency Model. Structurally, the competency model consists of three components—domains (which in this case

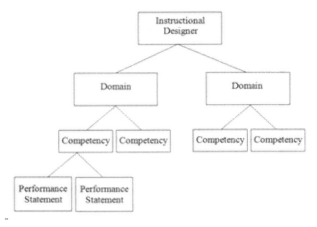

Figure 1.2.   Structure of the ibstpi competency model for the instructional designer.

primarily follow the design process), competencies, and performance statements (see Figure 1.2 above)

Domains are clusters of related competencies. This categorization serves to establish the relationship between competencies according to larger areas of activities. In the ibstpi Instructional Designer Competency model, the competencies have been grouped in five domains: ***professional foundations***, ***analysis and planning***, ***design and development***, ***implementation and evaluation***, and ***management***.

Competencies are the core component of the ibstpi model. They are short statements, each one providing a general description of a complex effort. In the ***planning and analysis*** domain, for example there are four competencies: (1) Conduct a needs assessment in order to recommend appropriate design solutions and strategies, (2) Identify and describe target population and environmental characteristics, (3) Select and use analysis techniques for determining instructional content, and (4) Analyze the characteristics of existing and emerging technologies and their potential use.

Each competency is supported by a list of performance statements which provide a fuller description of how the competency is demonstrated. For example, the three performance statements supporting the competency, ***Analyze the characteristics of existing and emerging technologies and their potential uses***, include (a) Describe the capabilities of existing and emerging technologies required to enhance the impact of instruction, (b) Evaluate the capacity of given instructional and learning environments to support selected technologies, and (c) Assess the benefits and limitations of existing and emerging technologies. The performance statements are not procedural steps, rather they are elaborations of the competency statement in behavioral and measurable terms.

The competencies and their respective performance statements were originally presented in 1986 as core ID competencies—those that enable a skilled designers to enter an organization and complete the basic instructional systems design process. There was an implicit assumption that these were fundamental sills of a trained, but novice designer. The updated competencies in 2000 did not follow this same model. Rather, the competencies were more comprehensive, encompassing those skills, knowledge, and attitudes essential for all designers, novice and advanced. In this edition, a new level of classification was added. Given the growing role of manager of an instructional design function and projects new competencies and performance statements were added to address managerial tasks. It is therefore critical that managers have essential (basic) instructional design competencies as well as advanced design competencies to effectively manage, advise on, and defend projects. They also should demonstrate managerial competencies to effectively perform the scope of a managerial job.

IMPLEMENTING THE MODEL FOR INSTRUCTIONAL DESIGNERS

The ibstpi competency development model is the key driver to the competency development process used when developing diverse job role competencies. It has been used for the initial development of instructional designer competencies (Richey et al., 2001), training manager competencies (Foxon et al., 2003), instructor competencies (Klein, Spector, Grabowski, & de la Teja, 2004), and evaluator competencies (Russ-Eft et al., 2008). Operationally, the use of the competency development models can be summed up by three phases, each of which is fundamentally an empirical procedure: (1) identification of foundational research, (2) competency drafting, and (3) competency validation and rewriting. These are briefly described below.

Phase 1: Identification of foundational research. The foundation of the ibstpi Instructional Designer Competency model was based on an extensive review of research and practice literature and programs, courses, and training modules in instructional design provided by universities and professional associations from around the world. In this revision effort information was sought primarily on changes in the instructional design field over the last decade. Information was sought on new ID roles, theories, models, and uses of technologies in instruction. An independent literature review and survey study sought information from ID graduates who are actively working in the ID field (e.g., business and industry, higher education, K-12, etc.) to identify new behaviors, values, ethical concerns, and future visions for instruction design field. This survey study recommended additional focus on areas of human performance, ID function management, and technology integration competencies, for example, that were not covered in the 2000 ID standards.

Phase 2: Competency drafting. The base list of competencies was analyzed and debated by ibstpi board of directors with particular expertise in different specialty areas of instructional design. Additional competencies and performance statements were added to better articulate the competencies of different levels of instructional designers. Some competencies were slightly restated and reorganized to clarify new roles of the instructional designer, suggesting career progression. A new classification level was also added based on the emerging role of the ID function manager and increased importance of managing ID functions and projects noted from the survey study and new literature. Experts in instructional design from outside ibstpi also reviewed and commented on the updated competencies and performance statements. These data were used to prepare a revised set of ID competencies for validation.

Phase 3: Competency validation and rewriting. Once a final draft of the statements was created in Phase 2, the statements were prepared to be sent out through a variety of academic, professional, and international associations, and private lists for validation by ID practitioners, researchers, and scholars around the world. A validation instrument was designed, developed, pilot tested, and administered worldwide via the web. The instrument asked about the criticality of each competency and performance statement and provided for open-ended comments. The results validated the competency set and provided suggestions for minor adjustments to the set of standards.

Once the minor adjustment were discussed, approved by the team, and implemented, a second survey was created to identify the level of classification of each statement as essential, advanced, or managerial. This survey was sent to acknowledged experts in the ID field. The results solidified the classification for each competency and performance statement.

Additional comments from both surveys and additional board of director reviews provided feedback on how to describe some of the more complex or generic statements. These data were collected and used to create narrative descriptions of the competencies and performance statements provided in Chapter 3.

Once the competencies and performance statements were finalized and classified, as per ibstpi policy, the final set of ID competencies was submitted to the entire ibstpi board for discuss and vote as to whether the updates adhere to ibstpi's mission, vision, and values. The board approved the set and this book was planned. Details on the entire process for validating the instructional designer competencies can be found in Chapter 6.

ASSUMPTIONS UNDERLYING IBSTPI THE ID COMPETENCIES

The ibstpi ID competencies are based upon some general assumptions which are critical to understanding the competencies and their use.

> **Assumption 1**. Instructional designers are those persons who demonstrate instructional design competencies on the job regardless of their job title or training.

Even though most experienced designers take it for granted that people are clear as to who designers are, in some situations that distinction may not be completely obvious. Certainly many designers have acquired their skills on the job or by attending short workshops, rather than by completing formal academic programs and earning an advanced degree. Likewise, many organizations do not have a formal job title of instructional designer. For some the *trainer* is both a designer of instruction as well as a deliverer of instruction. For some, the *performance technologist* assumes instructional design responsibilities. Sometimes it is the *human resources generalist or specialist* who assumes the roles of an instructional designer. In K-12 and higher education it is often the *teachers, curriculum developers*, and *faculty* who assume instructional design responsibilities.

Designers also assume specialized roles. Seniors designers, for example, may serve as the project manager, but are still considered a designer even with the expanded role. This is one reason it is critical that instructional project managers have strong ID competencies. Others designers may concentrate on only one phase of the process, for example needs assessment or evaluation. While it is not unusual for a designer to perform development tasks as well, those who concentrate totally on development or production tasks are **not** generally considered designers. For example, graphic artists and programmers may be critical members of a design team, but they are not instructional designers nor are they likely to have design competencies.

The ibstpi competencies pertain to persons whose job encompasses any portion of the primary design domains. In other words, if one's work pertains to planning and analysis, design and development, implementation and evaluation, and project management for a instructional project, that person is considered to be an instructional designer subject to these competencies, except as noted in the description of developers above.

Whether a designer performs his or her job in a skillful manner is not relevant to one's general classification as a designer. Consequently, these competencies can pertain to a wide variety of persons and jobs.

Assumption 2. ID Competencies pertain to persons working in a wide range of job settings.

Practicing designers have many job titles and work in many settings. This phenomenon has occurred as instructional design and training positions have grown and become more sophisticated over the years. The work environment often shapes design practice. For example, designers working as external consultants frequently have little to do with product implementation or maintenance. At times, they do not even engage in summative evaluation activities. On the other hand, designers working in a given organization (as an internal consultant) are likely to be very involved in program maintenance, in summative evaluation, and often conducting impact evaluations. The ibstpi competencies are applicable to each of these situations.

One point must be highlight however. While the ibstpi ID competencies are not specifically designed as applying only to business applications of instructional design, there is an emphasis on issues and processes more unique to a business environment than those of K-12 schools or of higher education or community-based education. For example, creating cost-benefit business cases or managing large design teams. This emphasis reflects where the predominance of design work currently takes place. The business orientation is more obvious in the implementation and management domain. Nonetheless, it is not difficult to use the competencies in any setting. Case in point, the ID practitioners who participated in the validation of this set of competencies were from business and industry, higher education, K-12, government and military, not-for-profit and other settings from around the world.

Assumption 3. ID Competencies define the manner in which design should be practiced.

Dick, Watson, and Kaufman (1981) contrasted two approaches to competency development—a consensus model that emphasized the "what is" and the model-building approach that focused on "what should be." While to a greater extent the ibstpi ID competencies represent a blend of these two approaches, the dominant orientation is the more idealized stance. There was a conscious effort to anticipate the needs for the future, and to establish standards for expert behavior that will advance the field. Consequently, it is possible for some designers to find elements of the new list that are unfamiliar to them. The difficult part of the task was to create competencies that are idealistic in nature and still practical and useable in actual work environments.

To a great extent the expanding theoretical foundations of instructional design guided this tasks. The 1986 ID competencies were directed primarily by general systems theory and to a great extent behavioral learning theory. The 2000 updated competencies maintain the systems theory influence and reflects cognitive theory and those theory bases associated with performance improvement. This 2012 version reflects the past foundations and philosophical views of ID practitioners (Sheehan & Johnson, 2011), new social aspects of team collaborations (Reiser & Dempsey, 2007; Staley & Ice, 2009), influences of emerging technologies on design and development (Koszalka & Ntloedibe-Kuswani, 2010; McDonald & Gibbons, 2009), the expanding practice role of designers in multiple contexts and domains (Cristensen & Osguthorpe, 2004), and changes in the technology sophistication of target learners (Sims & Koszalka, 2008).

> **Assumption 4.** Instructional design is a process most commonly guided by systematic design models and principles.

In the early days of instructional design adherence to a systematic approach to design was typically assumed. Diversity has come with the growth of the field. Today alternative design paradigms are being used. Visscher-Voerman, Gustafson, and Plomp (1999) described three additional paradigms—communicative, pragmatic, and artistic. The communicative paradigm emphasizes reaching consensus among these parties throughout the design process. The pragmatic paradigm is distinguished by repeated try-out and revision based upon stakeholder's perceptions. The artistic paradigm (typical of many technology-based design and development projects) relies on the developer's own subjective criteria, as well as those of the client.

Nonetheless, the ibstpi competencies are firmly rooted in a belief that the majority of ID practice is still dominated by traditional instructional systems design (ISD) models (see Gustafson & Branch, 2002), although many environments now emphasize different approaches and work focus (e.g., rapid prototyping, user-design). These models are exemplified by Dick, Carey, and Carey (2005), Morrison, Ross, and Kemp (2001), Seels and Glasgow (1997), Smith and Ragan (2005) or by similar models adapted specifically to business and other nonschool environments such as Rothwell and Kazanas (1998).

> **Assumption 5.** Instructional designer competence spans novice designers, advanced designers, and design managers.

The ID competencies were designed to be relevant to all levels of expertise. The 1986 competencies were presented as core competencies—those competencies that should be possessed by all those in ID roles. As such they summarized the essential competencies required successfully conduct in the instructional design process. A comparison of the 1986, 2000, and 2012 competencies shows that these core competencies still remain central to instructional design practices. However the current and changing complexities of the design field are not reflected in the older versions.

The current competency updating process started with an agreement among ibstpi directors that this list was to be a comprehensive compilation of the current competencies viewed as core to all and those of advanced instructional designers and design function managers. In support of this further classification of expertise is a body of literature that provides a credible definition of design expertise (e.g., see Ertmer, York, & Gedik, 2009; Eseryel, 2006; Hardré, Ge, & Thomas, 2006; LeMaistre, 1998; Perez & Emery, 1995; Rowland, 1992). In addition, the strong emphasis in the field on distributed teams (Eseryel, 2006; Koszalka & Wu, 2010) and the use of new and emerging technologies and social media have suggested that designers enhance their competencies based in communication skills, technology knowledge and skills, and new social learning theories influencing learning and instructional theories (see Jacobson, 2008; Rogers, Graham, & Mayes, 2007; van Merriënboer & Martens, 2011).

> **Assumption 6:** ID competencies should be meaningful and useful to designers worldwide.

Given that instructional design is a global activity, there was a conscious effort to construct new competencies in such a way that they were applicable to designers working in many countries and many cultures. This has been done to make each competency and performance statement culturally sensitive, as much as possible. Terminology was modified to remove language unique to the United State's design environment. The validation process sought feedback from design practitioners, instructional design scholars, and internationally educated designers from around the globe.

> **Assumption 7:** ID competencies are generic and amenable to customization.

The application of ibstpi competencies is broad. ID competencies have been constructed so that they speak to generic design issues, and may lack dominant focus of a particular organization or industry. However, the competencies can be customized to meet unique characteristics of an organization. Friedlander (1996) suggested that this be accomplished by identifying, documenting, and prioritizing those competencies that are important to the success of the organization and then determining how it will measure each competency. Language may also be modified to incorporate terminology unique to the organization or the target industry.

Assumption 8. ID competencies reflect societal and disciplinary values and ethics.

The ibstpi competencies reflect trends, emerging issues, and particular philosophies of the times in which the specific model was built. While there was a conscious effort to develop competencies that do not espouse disciplinary biases, competencies are nonetheless influenced by the context in which they were devised. They are shaped by the forces operating within a field and by the larger context in which one works. The values of society at large impact competency construction. For example, there is a current societal emphasis on cultural diversity and accommodating to persons with a wide range of backgrounds and abilities. Not surprisingly, this force influenced the working of the new ID competencies. The incorporation of societal values is not seen as a deficiency, rather as one way in which a list of competencies serves as an expression of ideal behavior—the standards to which we as designers should aspire.

Assumption 9: Instructional design is most commonly seen as resulting in transfer of training and organizational improvement.

As the field of instructional design has grown, the prevailing view of the products of design efforts have also changed. Early models simple portrayed the product as an instructional program or material. The more appropriate outcome then was seen as learning, typically in the form of knowledge and skill acquisition. Today the outcome is largely viewed as transfer of training at the least and more characterized as individual performance improvement and organizational change at best. This latter view serves as a foundation for this version of the ID competencies.

The broad performance improvement stance expands the theoretical foundations of the competencies. The foundational design theory bases now includes theories that explain the nature of organizations, human motivation, psychometrics, ergonomics, and change (Rosenberg, Coscarelli, & Hutchison, 1999).

Assumption 10: Few instructional designers, regardless of their level of expertise, are able to successfully demonstrate all ID competencies.

The very comprehensive nature of the 2012 ibstpi ID competencies makes it unlikely that most designers, even those with substantial work experience, will be able to demonstrate each and every competency and performance statement. This is consistent with today's instructional design practice that is more complex and sophisticated than was in design practices even 10 years ago. To some extent, this reflects the emergence of areas of design specialization that have evolved with many design practitioners assuming distinct roles that are directed toward parts of the design process and with team approaches engaging instructional designers with different skill sets. In other cases, the apparent specialization is more indicative of the particular emphasis that naturally occurs in some work environments. Nonetheless, one should not be surprised if all designers can not demonstrate all the competencies, or all aspects of a given competency.

AN OVERVIEW OF THE ID COMPETENCY DISCUSSION

The remainder Part I is a detailed examination of the new ID competencies themselves. This includes Chapters 2-5.

Chapter 2 includes a complete list of competencies and performance statements.

Chapter 3 explores the dimensions and implications of each competency and its supporting performance statements. Narrative is provided to describe each competency and performance statement in detail.

Chapter 4 consists of an examination of the various way in which the competencies can be used by designers working in a variety of situations. The focus is on ID practitioners, ID (or training) managers and administrators, ID-oriented academics, and Associations that offer instructional design-related professional development.

Chapter 5 examines the ID competencies as they relate to key ID roles and specializations—the general ID practitioner, design function manager, analyst/evaluator, and technology specialists.

Part II of the book provides a report of the competency validation study. The data that served as the basis for revising and finalizing the competencies and performance statements are presented and discussed. These data establish the underlying integrity of the ibstpi ID competencies. This section may appeal only to those interested in ID research.

The Epilogue discusses future ibstpi efforts in competency development pertinent to instructional design and related areas.

The appendixes present additional documents that can facilitate one's understanding and uses for the new ID competencies. A list of references cited in the book, a copy of the previous competencies and performance statements, a glossary of key ID terms, and copy of the ibstpi code of ethical standards are all provided. These materials may be useful to those wishing to expand their knowledge of instructional design and its applicability to their work.

CHAPTER 2

INSTRUCTIONAL DESIGNER COMPETENCIES AND PERFORMANCE STATEMENTS*

There are 22 newly updated ibstpi instructional designer competencies. These competencies are clustered into 5 domains and are supported by 105 performance statements. The domain groupings serve organizational and conceptual functions and suggest the scope and interrelatedness of the instructional designer's job tasks.

In each of the five domains there are specific skills and knowledge that every instructional designer is expected to master (labeled as *essential*), skills and knowledge that the most experienced and expert designers would be expected to master (labeled as *advanced*), and new to this set, the skills and knowledge that a manager of a design function or instructional project would be expected to master (labeled as *managerial*). These competencies reflect the fact that the field of instructional design has grown in breadth, depth, and complexity such that no one person can be expected to be fully competent in all related skills and knowledge.

*The Instructional Designer Competencies and Performance Statements are copyrighted and wholly owned by the International Board of Standards for Training, Performance and Instruction (ibstpi).

Instructional Designer Competencies: The Standards, Fourth Edition, pp. 23–30
Copyright © 2013 by Information Age Publishing
All rights of reproduction in any form reserved.

THE INSTRUCTIONAL DESIGNER COMPETENCIES AND PERFORMANCE STATEMENTS (2012)

PROFESSIONAL FOUNDATIONS

1. Communicate effectively in visual, oral and written form (*essential*).

   (a) Write and edit messages that are clear, concise, and grammatically correct (*essential*).

   (b) Deliver presentations that effectively engage audiences and communicate clear messages (*essential*).

   (c) Use active listening skills (*essential*).

   (d) Solicit, accept, and provide constructive feedback (*essential*).

   (e) Present written and oral messages that take into account the type of information being delivered and the diverse backgrounds, roles, and varied responsibilities of the audience (*advanced*).

   (f) Facilitate meetings effectively (*advanced*).

   (g) Use effective collaboration and consensus-building skills (*advanced*).

   (h) Use effective negotiation and conflict resolution skills (*advanced*).

   (i) Use effective questioning techniques (*advanced*).

   (j) Disseminate status, summary, or action-oriented reports (*advanced*).

2. Apply research and theory to the discipline of instructional design. (*advanced*).

   (a) Explain key concepts and principles related to instructional design (*essential*).

   (b) Apply systems thinking to instructional design and performance improvement projects (*essential*).

   (c) Apply results of instructional design research, theory, and practice (*advanced*).

   (d) Promote how instructional design research, theory, and practice literature may affect design practices in a given situation (*advanced*).

   (e) Apply concepts, techniques, and theories of other disciplines to learning and performance improvement (*advanced*).

3. Update and improve knowledge, skills, and attitudes pertaining to the instructional design process and related fields *(essential)*.

   (a) Participate in professional development activities *(essential)*.
   (b) Establish and maintain contacts with other professionals *(essential)*.
   (c) Acquire and apply new technology skills in instructional design practice *(essential)*.
   (d) Document and disseminate work as a foundation for future efforts, publications, or professional presentations *(advanced)*.

4. Apply data collection and analysis skills in instructional design projects *(advanced)*.

   (a) Identify the data to be collected *(advanced)*.
   (b) Use a variety of data collection tools and procedures *(essential)*.
   (c) Apply appropriate data collection methodologies to needs assessment and evaluation *(advanced)*.
   (d) Use appropriate quantitative and/or qualitative analysis procedures in needs assessment and evaluation *(advanced)*.

5. Identify and respond to ethical, legal, and political implications of design in the workplace *(essential)*.

   (a) Identify ethical, legal, and political dimensions of instructional design practice and instructional products *(advanced)*.
   (b) Plan for and respond to ethical, legal, and political consequences of design decisions *(advanced)*.
   (c) Recognize and respect the intellectual property rights of others *(essential)*.
   (d) Adhere to regulatory guidelines and organizational policies *(essential)*.
   (e) Comply with organizational and professional codes of ethics *(essential)*.

PLANNING AND ANALYSIS

6. Conduct a needs assessment in order to recommend appropriate design solutions and strategies *(advanced)*.

   (a) Identify varying perceptions of need among stakeholders and the implications of those perceptions *(advanced)*.

(b) Describe the nature of a learning or performance problem *(essential)*.

(c) Determine the root causes of identified discrepancies *(advanced)*.

(d) Synthesize findings to identify and recommend potential instructional and noninstructional solutions *(advanced)*.

(e) Estimate costs and benefits of possible solutions *(advanced)*.

(f) Prepare and disseminate a needs assessment report *(advanced)*.

7. Identify and describe target population and environmental characteristics *(essential)*.

(a) Determine characteristics of the target population that may impact the design and delivery of instruction *(essential)*.

(b) Determine characteristics of the physical, social, political, and cultural environment that may influence learning, attitudes, and performance *(advanced)*.

(c) Identify the infrastructure that is available to support the design and delivery of instruction *(advanced)*.

(d) Determine the extent to which organizational mission, philosophy, and values may impact the design and delivery of instruction *(advanced)*.

(e) Analyze, evaluate, and use learner profile data and environmental characteristics to design instruction *(essential)*.

8. Select and use analysis techniques for determining instructional content *(essential)*.

(a) Identify the scope of required content in accordance with needs assessment findings *(essential)*.

(b) Elicit, synthesize, and validate content from subject matter experts *(essential)*.

(c) Analyze existing instructional products to determine adequacy or inadequacy of content, instruction, and learning *(essential)*.

(d) Determine the breadth and depth of intended content coverage given instructional constraints *(essential)*.

(e) Determine subordinate and prerequisite skills and knowledge *(essential)*.

(f) Use appropriate techniques to analyze various types and sources of content *(essential)*.

9. Analyze the characteristics of existing and emerging technologies and their potential use *(essential)*.

   (a) Describe the capabilities of existing and emerging technologies required to enhance the impact of instruction *(essential)*.

   (b) Evaluate the capacity of given instructional and learning environments to support selected technologies *(advanced)*.

   (c) Assess the benefits and limitations of existing and emerging technologies *(advanced)*.

DESIGN AND DEVELOPMENT

10. Use an instructional design and development process appropriate for a given project *(essential)*.

    (a) Select or create an instructional design process based the nature of the project *(essential)*.

    (b) Modify the instructional design process as project parameters change *(advanced)*.

    (c) Describe a rationale for the selected, created or modified instructional design process *(advanced)*.

11. Organize instructional programs and/or products to be designed, developed, and evaluated *(essential)*.

    (a) Determine the overall scope of instructional programs and/or products *(advanced)*.

    (b) Identify and sequence instructional goals *(essential)*.

    (c) Specify and sequence the anticipated learning and performance outcomes *(essential)*.

12. Design instructional interventions *(essential)*.

    (a) Identify instructional strategies that align with instructional goals and anticipated learning outcomes *(essential)*.

    (b) Apply appropriate interaction design and interactive learning principles *(essential)*.

    (c) Use appropriate message and visual design principles *(essential)*.

    (d) Apply appropriate motivational design principles *(essential)*

    (e) Accommodate social, cultural, political, and other individual factors that may influence learning *(essential)*.

(f) Select appropriate technology and media to enhance instructional interventions, taking into account theory, research, and practical factors *(essential)*.

13. Plan noninstructional interventions *(advanced)*.

(a) Identify which, if any, noninstructional interventions are appropriate (e.g., performance support, knowledge management, personnel selection, job redesign, incentive systems) *(advanced)*.

(b) Justify why noninstructional interventions are appropriate *(advanced)*.

(c) Create design specifications for noninstructional interventions *(advanced)*.

14. Select or modify existing instructional materials *(essential)*.

(a) Identify and select materials that support the content analyses, proposed technologies, delivery methods, and instructional strategies *(essential)*.

(b) Conduct cost-benefit analyses to decide whether to use or modify existing materials *(advanced)*.

(c) Validate selection or modification of existing instruction *(advanced)*.

(d) Integrate existing instructional materials into the design *(essential)*.

(e) Develop instructional materials *(essential)*.

15. Develop specifications that serve as the basis for media production *(essential)*.

(a) Produce instructional materials in a variety of delivery formats *(essential)*.

(b) Develop materials that align with the content analyses, proposed technologies, delivery methods, and instructional strategies *(essential)*.

(c) Collaborate with production specialists *(essential)*.

16. Design learning assessment *(advanced)*.

(a) Identify the learning processes and outcomes to be measured *(essential)*.

(b) Construct reliable and valid methods of assessing learning and performance *(advanced)*.

(c) Ensure that assessment is aligned with instructional goals, anticipated learning outcomes, and instructional strategies *(essential)*.

EVALUATION AND IMPLEMENTATION

17. Evaluate instructional and noninstructional interventions. *(advanced)*

   (a) Design evaluation plans *(advanced)*.
   (b) Implement formative evaluation plans *(essential)*.
   (c) Implement summative evaluation plans *(essential)*.
   (d) Prepare and disseminate evaluation report *(advanced)*.

18. Revise instructional and noninstructional solutions based on data. *(essential)*.

   (a) Identify product and program revisions based on review of evaluation data *(advanced)*.
   (b) Revise the delivery process based on evaluation data *(essential)*.
   (c) Revise products and programs based on evaluation data *(essential)*.

19. Implement, disseminate, and diffuse instructional and noninstructional interventions *(advanced)*.

   (a) Create a vision of change that aligns learning and performance goals with organizational goals *(managerial)*.
   (b) Plan for the implementation of the interventions *(advanced)*.
   (c) Plan for the dissemination of the interventions *(managerial)*.
   (d) Plan for the diffusion of the interventions *(managerial)*.
   (e) Disseminate the interventions *(advanced)*.
   (f) Monitor implementation, dissemination, and diffusion progress *(managerial)*.
   (g) Identify required modifications to implementation, dissemination, and diffusion processes *(advanced)*.

MANAGEMENT

20. Apply business skills to managing the instructional design function *(managerial)*.

    (a) Align instructional design efforts with organization's strategic plans and tactics *(managerial)*.
    (b) Establish standards of excellence for the instructional design function *(managerial)*.
    (c) Develop a business case to promote the critical role of the instructional design function *(managerial)*.
    (d) Recruit, retain, and develop instructional design personnel *(managerial)*.
    (e) Develop financial plans and controls for the instructional design function *(managerial)*.
    (f) Obtain and maintain management and stakeholder support for the design function *(managerial)*.
    (g) Market instructional design services and manage customer relations *(managerial)*.

21. Manage partnerships and collaborative relationships *(managerial)*.

    (a) Identify stakeholders and the nature of their involvement *(advanced)*.
    (b) Build and promote effective relationships between the design team and stakeholders *(managerial)*.
    (c) Manage cross functional teams *(managerial)*.
    (d) Conduct project reviews with design team members and stakeholders *(managerial)*.

22. Plan and manage instructional design projects *(advanced)*.

    (a) Establish project scope and goals *(advanced)*.
    (b) Write proposals for instructional design projects *(advanced)*.
    (c) Use a variety of planning and management tools for instructional design projects *(advanced)*.
    (d) Allocate resources to support the project plan *(managerial)*.
    (e) Manage multiple priorities to maintain project time line *(managerial)*.
    (f) Identify and resolve project issues *(managerial)*.

CHAPTER 3

THE INSTRUCTIONAL DESIGNER COMPETENCIES

Discussion and Analysis

DISCUSSION AND ANALYSIS INTRODUCTION

The substantially expanded content in the updated ibstpi Instructional Designer competencies reflects the current complexity of instructional design praxis (see, e.g., Richey, Klein, & Tracey, 2011) The following discussion presents a rationale and explanation of each domain, competency, and performance statement in this new list. Attention is especially drawn to the novel and broadened competencies. The rationale and perspectives presented here reflect the prevalent and prominent views of the international instructional design community as articulated during the updating and vetting process for these standards. The five domains and their components present an integrated account of the knowledge, skills, and attitudes that instructional designer professionals should possess, at various levels, to be competent performers.

PROFESSIONAL FOUNDATIONS

The first competency domain is Professional Foundations, and it pertains to five competency areas:

- Effective communications
- Application of research and theory
- Updating and improving personal competence
- Applying data collection and analysis skills
- Responding to ethical, legal, and political implications of design

This competency domain is an explicit recognition of the current professional status of the instructional design field. As with any profession, this status has associated obligations and expectations. These obligations and expectations range from clear and coherent communication skills to responsibility for advancing the profession and advancing within the profession.

1. Communicate effectively in visual, oral and written form. (essential) This is an *essential* competency and it includes ten performance statements, four essential and six advanced.

    (a) Write and edit messages that are clear, concise, and grammatically correct *(essential)*.

    (b) Deliver presentations that effectively engage audiences and communicate clear messages *(essential)*.

    (c) Use active listening skills *(essential)*.

    (d) Solicit, accept, and provide constructive feedback *(essential)*.

    (e) Present written and oral messages that take into account the type of information being delivered and the diverse backgrounds, roles, and varied responsibilities of the audience *(advanced)*.

    (f) Facilitate meetings effectively *(advanced)*.

    (g) Use effective collaboration and consensus-building skills *(advanced)*.

    (h) Use effective negotiation and conflict resolution skills *(advanced)*.

    (i) Use effective questioning techniques *(advanced)*.

    (j) Disseminate status, summary, or action-oriented reports *(advanced)*.

One of the most essential skills instructional designers must possess is the ability to communicate effectively. It occurs at every phase of the design process, from needs assessment through implementation and dissemination of solutions. Moreover, during most phases of the design process, designers are interacting with a variety of individuals, including clients, subject matter experts, other designers, media production personnel, and learners. Regardless of the role these individuals are playing in a particular project, the designer must be able to communicate effectively with them.

Instructional designers must be able to communicate effectively in visual, oral and written forms. The artifacts designers produce often are in the form of instructional materials, presentations, and reports, as well as brief messages to others involved in the design project. Regardless of the form, it is important for the designer to be able to communicate clearly and concisely, adjusting the nature of the message according to the needs and interests of the intended audience.

Communication skills for instructional designers go far beyond just being able to share and present information. For example, designers must be able to gather information from clients, subject matter experts, and learners, work effectively with other members of the design team, and gain and maintain support from key administrators. To do so, designers must possess a strong set of listening and questioning skills. The ability to facilitate discussion, with individuals and with groups, is also an essential skill. The latter is particularly important because instructional designers often are called upon to run or facilitate group meetings.

Instructional designers frequently work with others who have different roles and responsibilities within an organization and whose perspectives on an issue may differ from that of the instructional designer and/or other members of the design team. That being the case, instructional designers must also be skilled at negotiating and resolving conflicts, as well as facilitating collaboration and building consensus. Being able to do so effectively also requires instructional designers to be skilled at providing feedback as well as soliciting feedback from others and using that feedback to improve the quality of their own work.

2. Apply research and theory to the discipline of instructional design. (advanced) This is an ***advanced*** competency and it includes five performance statements, two essential and three advanced.

   (a) Explain key concepts and principles related to instructional design *(essential)*.

   (b) Apply systems thinking to instructional design and performance improvement projects *(essential)*.

(c) Apply results of instructional design research, theory, and practice *(advanced)*.

(d) Promote how instructional design research, theory, and practice literature may affect design practices in a given situation *(advanced)*.

(e) Apply concepts, techniques, and theories of other disciplines to learning and performance improvement *(advanced)*.

Starting in the mid-1960s, with the publication of works by pioneering figures in the field (e.g., Banathy, 1968; Gagne, 1965; Glaser, 1965), a great deal of literature about the instructional design process, and systems thinking as applied to instructional design, has been produced. Books and journal articles describing instructional design research, theories, and practices are abundant. Instructional designers at all levels of expertise should understand and be able to clearly describe the key concepts, principles, and practices described in that literature. Moreover, professionals in the instructional design field, particularly those at the advanced level, should be able to select and employ those principles and practices that may be applicable in a particular situation.

The ability to explain key concepts and principles in the field should also serve to help designers promote the proper use of those ideas. For instance, when faced with a learning or performance problem, instructional designers should not only be able to identify an appropriate approach to solving that problem (or example, by first conducting a needs assessment), they should also be able to describe the approach in manner that enables a client to recognize the value of employing it.

Familiarity with the major concepts, principles, and practices in the field should also serve to help instructional designers correct misperceptions about it. For example, a common criticism that is leveled against the instructional design process is that it is lock-step, linear approach. Whereas graphics of some instructional design models depict the process in that manner, designers who clearly understand the process should be able to describe the iterative, nonlinear nature of the instructional design approach.

Instructional designers, especially those at the advanced level, should not limit themselves to drawing upon literature within the instructional design field in order to inform their work. Research, theory, and practices in related fields such as organizational development, information technology, and the learning sciences can often serve to improve instructional design practices. Indeed, in recent years, special issues of several journals within the instructional design field have focused on related disciplines (e.g., the learning sciences special issue of *Educational Technology*, 2004, vol. 44, no. 3). Learning and performance problems are more likely to be solved if instructional designers possess the ability to employ concepts, techniques, and theories from related fields, as well as their own.

3. Update and improve knowledge, skills, and attitudes pertaining to the instructional design process and related fields (essential). This is an *essential* competency and it includes four performance statements, three essential and one advanced.

    (a) Participate in professional development activities *(essential)*.
    (b) Establish and maintain contacts with other professionals *(essential)*.
    (c) Acquire and apply new technology skills in instructional design practice *(essential)*.
    (d) Document and disseminate work as a foundation for future efforts, publications, or professional presentations *(advanced)*.

Over the history of the instructional design field, many of the core skills in the field have remained constant. However, over the past 2 decades two sets of developments related to the field have brought about a significant expansion in the range of skills and knowledge instructional designers are expected to possess. The first set of developments involves new views regarding the teaching and learning process, including the performance improvement movement, constructivist views of teaching and learning, and development of the learning sciences. The second set of developments involves major changes in how technology is being used to share information, present instruction, and facilitate learning. These changes include, among others, the increasing use of online learning technologies, performance support and knowledge management systems, social networking and game-based learning.

In light of the rapid changes that are taking place within the field, instructional designers can ill-afford to simply rely on the set of skills they learned when they first entered the profession. Instead, it is incumbent that designers engage in professional activities that will enhance, expand and build upon their existing knowledge base and skill set. There are a wide variety of ways designer can do so. Prominent among these is engaging in professional development activities such as participating in webinars and workshops.

Regularly interacting with other professionals in the field is another important means of updating professional skills and knowledge, and in most cases becoming active in a professional association is likely the best means of promoting this type of interaction. Such organizations offer a wide variety of professional development opportunities. By attending the conferences conducted by an association, reading the journals it produces, and joining and becoming active in one or more of the association's special interest groups and committees, instructional designers can expand their professional network and greatly enhance their skills and knowledge.

To further advance the field, it is also incumbent that instructional designers document and disseminate their work with others in the profession. Presenting papers at conferences, publishing papers in journals, and posting ideas or project designs to shared spaces online are three important means of sharing and discussing ideas with others. Professionals in the field should strive, preferably on at least an annual basis, to present papers at conferences or prepare manuscripts for publication in professional journals.

4. Apply data collection and analysis skills in instructional design projects *(advanced)*. This is an **advanced** competency and it includes four performance statements, one essential and three advanced.

    (a) Identify the data to be collected *(advanced)*.

    (b) Use a variety of data collection tools and procedures *(essential)*.

    (c) Apply appropriate data collection methodologies to needs assessment and evaluation *(advanced)*.

    (d) Use appropriate quantitative and/or qualitative analysis procedures in needs assessment and evaluation *(advanced)*.

Instructional design is an empirical process; it relies on the use of data that is collected through observation or experience. In other words, from beginning to end, many of the decisions that are made during the instructional design process are determined by the data that those involved in the process have gathered. In light of the importance of data uses during the instructional design process, it is essential that instructional designers have the skills necessary to correctly identify the types of data that must be collected, employ a variety of techniques tools and techniques to collect appropriate data, and use appropriate methods for analyzing that data.

Data collection and analysis procedures are particularly important at the outset of a design project, when an instructional designer is first attempting to ascertain the nature of a problem. Among the data-driven questions that need to be addressed at this stage of the process are what is current level of learning and/or performance among those in the target population, how does that compare with the desired level, and what are the likely causes for any discrepancies between the two? Designers must identify the techniques and tools for collecting data that answer such questions (e.g., via observations, interviews and surveys), must be adept at developing and using those tools and techniques, and must be able to analyze the data that is collected in order to make appropriate design decisions.

In a similar vein, data collection and analysis skills are essential during the evaluation phase of a design project. During this phase, designers need to determine whether the solutions that have been implemented have actually helped solve the learning and/or performance problems that were initially identified. In order to do so, the designers first need to identify the types of data to collect (oftentimes learning, performance and attitude data), and select, develop and implement the appropriate data collection tools and procedures (e.g., performance appraisals, written or oral assessments, attitude surveys, interviews, observations, etc.). Then designers must be able to employ the appropriate qualitative and/or quantitative analysis procedures (the latter often involving descriptive, rather than inferential, statistics) to determine the effectiveness of the solutions that were implemented.

5. Identify and respond to ethical, legal, and political implications of design in the workplace *(essential)*. This is an ***essential*** competency and it includes five performance statements, three essential and two advanced.

    (a) Identify ethical, legal, and political dimensions of instructional design practice and instructional products *(advanced)*.

    (b) Plan for and respond to ethical, legal, and political consequences of design decisions *(advanced)*.

    (c) Recognize and respect the intellectual property rights of others *(essential)*.

    (d) Adhere to regulatory guidelines and organizational policies *(essential)*.

    (e) Comply with organizational and professional codes of ethics *(essential)*.

Most of the professional associations in the instructional design field, as well as many of the organizations that employ instructional designers, have developed a set of ethical and legal codes that the members of the organization are expected to adhere to. ibstpi has developed a code of ethical standards for instructional designers that describes a set of professional behaviors that, when adhered to, should enable instructional designers to act in a ethical manner and, consequently, not engage in activities that result in the legal and moral issues that are likely to arise when a professional in the field engages in questionable activities. The ibstpi Ethical Standards fall into four categories: responsibilities to others, social mandates, respecting the rights of others, and professional practices (see Appendix D for a complete listing of these ethical standards).

Given current-day conditions, one of the many ibstpi standards that deserves special attention is that which indicates the importance of respecting the copyright and intellectual property rights of others. In an era where the Internet is regularly used to display and share a wide variety of types of intellectual property, and where tools for copying and editing such properties are abundant, copying and using the intellectual property of others, without first seeking and receiving their permission, has become an all-too-common activity. Those involved in the instructional design profession need to be acutely aware of the ethical and legal issues involved in undertaking this inappropriate activity and must avoid engaging in it.

The ethical standards developed by ibstpi address many of the same ethical and legal behaviors described in the standards put forth by other professional organizations in the instructional design field and are likely to be well-aligned with the ethical and legal practices organizations that hire instructional designers expect those designers to adhere to. It is essential that as they engage in their professional practices, instructional designers conduct their activities in accordance with those ethical and legal standards.

PLANNING AND ANALYSIS

While the professional development competencies establish ID as a profession, the four competencies in the planning and analysis domain describe some of the most basic skills of this profession. Many designers see their strongest attributes as their ability to systematically analyze a problem or situation and move toward a solution. There are four competencies in the domain of planning and analysis and twenty performance statements. These competencies represent critical components in the ID process. It is in this phase that the foundational data for the project is collected during a needs assessment, the general design of the program is determined, content is validated and organized, learners and learning and practice environments are analyzed, and technology use is determined. The four competences in the planning and analysis domain relate to:

- Conducting an needs assessment
- Describing audience and environmental characteristics
- Determining instructional content
- Analyzing potential technologies for use in instruction

One of the competencies is considered advanced and the remaining three are essential. Ten of the supporting performance statements are essential and ten are advanced. Therefore, advanced instructional designers should be able to demonstrate all of the competencies and new instructional designers should be able to demonstrate the essential performance statements, and develop the more advanced ones over time.

Typically, the performance of planning and analysis tasks requires interactions with content experts (CE) or subject matter expert (SME) since this is the stage in which the designer defines the content that will serve as the foundation of the final product. Acquiring and maintaining the following competencies in practices will likely assure quality instructional solution are recommended that will help close performance gaps identified during the needs assessment. The discussion of competencies six through nine and their accompanying performance statements follows.

6. Conduct a needs assessment in order to recommend appropriate design solutions and strategies *(advanced)*. This is an **advanced** competency and it includes six performance statements, one essential and five advanced.

   (a) Identify varying perceptions of need among stakeholders and the implications of those perceptions *(advanced)*.

   (b) Describe the nature of a learning or performance problem *(essential)*.

   (c) Determine the root causes of identified discrepancies *(advanced)*.

   (d) Synthesize findings to identify and recommend potential instructional and noninstructional solutions *(advanced)*.

   (e) Estimate costs and benefits of possible solutions *(advanced)*.

   (f) Prepare and disseminate a needs assessment report *(advanced)*.

The mixture of essential and advanced skills required in this competency is indicative of the complex nature of the needs assessment. Needs assessment in often carried out by a more advanced instructional designer, thus the classification of this competencies and all but one of its performance statements as advanced. All instructional designers should be able to describe the nature of performance problems, for example, what the performance is and should be, and how the performance gap is related to knowledge, skills, or attitudes. The five performance statements requiring advanced skills and knowledge are those where solutions are called for, and judgments and recommendation are made. In each case, poor decisions can have serious consequences on the final product.

Thus, instructional designers need to demonstrate a high level of design expertise (competence) when performing these tasks.

Needs assessment essentially responds to three questions—Where are we now? Where are we going? and How will we get there? It is a process of examining a perceived gap between an existing situation and those circumstances to which an organization aspire. It is a process that should result in identifying solutions to an organization's personnel performance problems.

The complexity of most organizations today require designers to conduct a correspondingly complex needs assessment, often addressing content dimensions and the nature of the learning and culture of the organization. Designer success is increasingly as dependent on being sensitive to the social morays and culture of an organization as it is having a strong knowledge of needs assessment tools and techniques. This is requisite to accurate identification and interpretation of organizational problems, and it is required in most circumstances to creatively select solutions to such problems.

Instructional designers are routinely expected to be able to differentiate between the need for instructional and noninstructional interventions, and select the most cost effective alternatives. Identifying root causes for performance problems thus is critical to these decisions. Today it is also critical that instructional designers be as familiar with noninstructional solutions (e.g., informational or knowledge-management systems, competency-position matching) and interventions as they are with traditional instructional solutions, since their goal is ultimately to improve on-the-job performance and help solve organizational performance problems.

7. Identify and describe target population and environmental characteristics (essential). This is an ***essential*** competency and it includes five performance statements, two are essential and three are advanced.

    (a) Determine characteristics of the target population that may impact the design and delivery of instruction *(essential)*.

    (b) Determine characteristics of the physical, social, political, and cultural environment that may influence learning, attitudes, and performance *(advanced)*.

    (c) Identify the infrastructure that is available to support the design and delivery of instruction *(advanced)*.

    (d) Determine the extent to which organizational mission, philosophy, and values may impact the design and delivery of instruction *(advanced)*.

(e) Analyze, evaluate, and use learner profile data and environmental characteristics to design instruction *(essential)*.

Again, the mixture of essential and advanced skills required in this competency is indicative of the complex nature of analyzing and describing performers and their work and learning environments. All designers should be able to competently determine the characteristics of the population and its impact of design and deliver of instructional solutions. Advanced designers are more likely to be competent in taking this analysis a step further because of their experience in determining less visible characteristics like political or social characteristics of the population and the philosophy and values of the organizational environment that will be a factor in designing and implementing instructional solutions. However, all levels of instructional designers should be competence in using and analyzing learner and environmental condition profile data to scope and recommend instructional design solutions.

Most target populations for instructional solutions are more diverse than was typical in the past. There are ranges of cultural and educational background, as well as age groups represented in organizational and educational settings. With a wavering economy many experienced workers, for example are being prepared for new positions which require new skills and knowledge. These workplace economic fluctuations and increases in globalization (e.g., multicultural workforce) exacerbate these conditions and make it more essential that instructional designer accommodate these complexities into any needs assessment recommendations. No longer is it important to just identify learner's prerequisite skills when identifying learning gaps and potential solutions, the instructional designer must account for more organizational performance factors.

Learner analysis skills are deceptively complex and extremely important to both short- and long-term success of any design project. When identifying the characteristics of the audience, designers are confronted with a unique challenge. They must determine the characteristics of the target learners and they must know which of these characteristics are critical to the success of the instruction and which impact learning. It is even more difficult to select those characteristics that influence the transfer of new knowledge and skills to work place performance. So, even though all designers must be able to gather learner data, it is typically up to the advanced designs to work with such data and decide what it critical to a given project.

This competency also speaks to the tasks of identifying environmental characteristics of the performers. These characteristic are critical to designing, developing, and implementing successful training. It speaks to the importance of the organization's physical (and virtual) dimensions and its culture. When instructional design is oriented towards performance improvement (rather than knowledge acquisition), the issues raised by these performance statements become critical.

Successful designers have long recognized the importance of careful analysis of both physical and social aspects of the instructional environment, and the cost of neglecting them. Factors such as lighting, air conditioning and heating, equipment and technology, comfort, and refreshments, among other environmental factors, al contribute to training and learning success. However, disciplinary research has also verified other environmental conditions that are critical to the ID process. An organization's culture, mission, vision, and value all influence training success, as they show support or lack of support for performer professional development. The degree of supervisory and coworker support, for example, exerts great influence on the extent to which newly acquired knowledge and skills are indeed transferred to the workplace.

Performance improvement interventions (e.g., instruction, noninstructional) are typically ineffective when the organization have not been thoroughly and accurately analyzed, and the data from such analysis have not been factored into the design and delivery of instruction. While novice designers should be able to deal with the physical dimensions of the instructional environment, advanced designers have a much higher probability of success when dealing with organizational climate factors. As with complexities of incorporating learner data into designs, it seems to take a more advanced designer to address the psychological aspects of a work climate in a training (or virtual training) design.

8. Select and use analysis techniques for determining instructional content *(essential)*. This is an ***essential*** competency and it includes six performance statements, all six are essential.

   (a) Identify the scope of required content in accordance with needs assessment findings *(essential)*.

   (b) Elicit, synthesize, and validate content from subject matter experts *(essential)*.

   (c) Analyze existing instructional products to determine adequacy or inadequacy of content, instruction, and learning *(essential)*.

   (d) Determine the breadth and depth of intended content coverage given instructional constraints *(essential)*.

   (e) Determine subordinate and prerequisite skills and knowledge *(essential)*.

   (f) Use appropriate techniques to analyze various types and sources of content *(essential)*.

This competency is focused upon content identification, a critical aspect of planning and analysis. It is a process that is essential for each design project. Consequently, basic skills in content identification are essential to all designers. Content must reflect needs assessment data, to be classified as instructional or prerequisite, and to be specified in a manner that is appropriate for the skill level and background of target audience. There are a variety of techniques that can be used for content identification, and novice designers must have some familiarity with them.

Content identification can be complex. It may involved extensive work with experts in subjects quite unknown to the designer. This demands essential skills, and experiences, in questioning and extracting information from persons who may have difficulty describing what they know well in terms that the uninitiated may have difficulty understanding. Content identification can also involve eliminating the nice-to-know information so that the instruction may highlight the need-to-know content. This is typically a process of very precisely analyzing and understanding organizational and learner needs to that content truly unnecessary can be eliminated. These essential content identification skills require designers to engage in high level cognitive processing. They often involve detailed analyzed, complex synthesis, and validating one's own conclusions.

9.   Analyze the characteristics of existing and emerging technologies and their potential use *(essential)*. This is an ***essential*** competency and it includes three performance statements, one essential and two advanced.

   (a)   Describe the capabilities of existing and emerging technologies required to enhance the impact of instruction *(essential)*.

   (b)   Evaluate the capacity of given instructional and learning environments to support selected technologies *(advanced)*.

   (c)   Assess the benefits and limitations of existing and emerging technologies *(advanced)*.

Unquestionably, the emergence of technologies into instruction and learning environments has exploded over the last decade. Even though computers were in use as far back as the 1986 version of the ID competencies, the role of technology has advanced far beyond the role of that time. This competency and its supporting performance statements reflects these advancements and the fact that it is now almost universally expected that designers have proficiency in a variety of technologies. It is important to remember however, that the focus of these competencies are on design. Technology use is a decision based on the design of instruction aimed at closing a performance gap. Knowledge of technology features is critical to design. The skills of programming and developing technology solutions are more in the purview of a programmer, developer, or information technology specialist—these roles have different competencies that can be guided by instructional designers in the creation of technology-based instruction or learning environments.

As indicated in the competency statement, all designers should have knowledge of the uses and benefits of classes of technology (e.g., learning management systems, digital tutorial systems, mobile technologies, hand-held devices. those technologies that are used in face-to-face and virtual situations) used regularly or with emerging uses in instructional situations. While designers may not be skilled in programming or coding with software, creating online applications, or producing video, for example, they should be able to select those technologies that will enhance a given design and provide technicians with the specifications for development. In many respects, this is the modern form of media selection.

Designers should also have the competencies to integrate technology in ways that facilitate individualized instruction, motivate learners, and that engage learners in creative and meaningful ways with content during instruction. Designers should be able to use technology to simulate and authentically present complex problem and decision-making situations. They are expected to use technology to facilitate learner involvement, even when instructors and content experts are separated by time, distance, and locations. They should be familiar with the different types of social (e.g., synchronous and asynchronous text, voice, and video) and collaborative (e.g., blogs, wikis, etc.) media. Designers should also know the limitations of technology and when it is not a cost-effect delivery solution.

Some designers are more knowledgeable and skilled than others with respect to operating technologies. Often these technology advanced designers go beyond merely creating simple instructional products and programs; they help to define and create the infrastructures that facilitates the use of technology in instruction. Networked environments (e.g., proprietary, intranet, Internet), for example, can be created and customized to provide opportunities for distance learning, just-in-time or on-demand training, and knowledge management. Advanced designers should have a competencies to evaluate the capacity of the learning environment to support selected technologies, for example, in the classroom, in virtual environments.

DESIGN AND DEVELOPMENT

It is not a surprise that instructional designers are expected to be able to design and develop instructional materials in a variety of formats. New technologies have led to a significant expansion of the field and at times to the development of new ID methodologies. However, as the discipline expands and as new technologies and methods are introduced, these fundamental design and development activities become more challenging and sophisticated. Nonetheless, at first glance the design and development competencies appear similar to, albeit expanded beyond, previous versions of the ID standards. The goal for the instructional designer is to maintain competency in the fundamental activities and thinking in design and development and expand the use of these practices as new technologies and methodologies emerge.

Although many basic design tasks remain fundamentally the same, the emergence of new ID techniques and technologies has somewhat blurred the definitions and boundaries between the tasks of instructional designers and information technologists or technology developers (often trained as programmers). Employers of instructional designers often expect their instructional designers to have advanced technology production skills and knowledge. The fundamental difference between the trained instructional designer and information technologists is that the latter often can create visually appealing resources however, often lack or have weaker competencies to design these resources as effective learning solutions. This set of standards clarifies the differences by providing a more concise list of performance statements to identify instructional design and development competencies while maintaining a perspective on the influences of new technologies and methodologies in practice. Thus, this update provides more specificity to clarify the breadth of design and development competencies and emphasize the importance of design over technology skills.

Also, given expanding roles of the instructional designer, a competency was added to address the growing role of instructional designer work on noninstructional interventions. Hypermedia and digital environments (e.g., Internet, social media tool) especially provide a platform for the design and development of informational, instructional, and learning resources (Grabowski & Small, 1997). Thus, instructional designers sometimes transform their role into an information technology or digital media development realm that is more informational and technology-skill focused rather than instructional. This design and development domain pertains to seven competency areas focused on instructional contexts.

- Use appropriate instructional design and development process
- Organize instructional projects
- Design instructional interventions
- Plan noninstructional interventions

- Select or modify existing interventions
- Develop instructional materials
- Design learning assessments

These competencies are essential at various degrees for all instructional designers and managers of instructional design projects. Based on the validation data collected, the international instructional design community are more convinced than ever that sound design and development principles are critical to successful instruction, especially given the plethora of new technologies that have emerged and seemingly taken center stage in many instructional environments. Acquiring and maintaining the following competencies in practices will likely assure quality instructional materials that are designed, developed, modified, and implemented using appropriate design methods and technologies.

10. Use an instructional design and development process appropriate for a given project *(essential)*. This is an ***essential*** competency and it includes three performance statements, one essential and two advanced.

    (a) Select or create an instructional design process based the nature of the project *(essential)*.

    (b) Modify the instructional design process as project parameters change *(advanced)*.

    (c) Describe a rationale for the selected, created or modified instructional design process *(advanced)*.

All instructional designers, from novice to manager, should be familiar with and able to participate in the systematic process of creating instruction. There are many generic and specialized process models (e.g., ADDIE, nonlinear ID, rapid development and prototyping, learner-centered design processes, user-design development process) that guide instructional designers and teams through identifying, designing, developing, implementing, evaluating, and continuously improving instruction (Gustafson & Branch, 2002). These models generally begin at the identification of a performance problem and end with implementation and evaluation of solutions. Each provides a systemic approach to creating instruction. Designers should have the competencies to carefully construct or select an appropriate process model based on the characteristics of the project and environment in which an instructional solution is being developed and implemented.

In most graduate programs that prepare instructional designers, students are taught a given design process model. Rarely are they encouraged to adapt or alter the model based on work settings or project variables. Some new designers become dismayed at the seeming lack of attention being paid to traditional ID models in the real world of work. In fact, many experienced designers are constantly adapting these procedures (or selecting a variety of alternative design models) to accommodate the idiosyncrasies of a particular project, particular client, or particular organization. Thus, advanced designers often competent in customizing generic design process models to meet project and environmental needs and then justify why they selected, modified, or created a new model. In a sense, they are marketing ID and educating others. If done well, this practice of adjusting models to project demands lays the foundation for project success.

11. Organize instructional programs and/or products to be designed, developed, and evaluated *(essential)*. This is an **essential** competency and it includes three performance statements, two essential and one advanced.

    (a) Determine the overall scope of instructional programs and/or products *(advanced)*.

    (b) Identify and sequence instructional goals *(essential)*.

    (c) Specify and sequence the anticipated learning and performance outcomes *(essential)*.

Organizing an instructional program should be based on findings from a needs assessment (e.g., performance problem identification, learning gap, content; see standards 6-9), instructional components recommended during the needs assessment (e.g., lecture, collaborative projects), and context for implementation (e.g., academic, business, on-the-job). Regardless of the particular technologies or the project thrust, designers organize instructional projects by defining program scope, setting instructional goals, and sequencing learning activities during the early design process stages.

Program scope is determined based on identified performance gap(s) and knowledge, skills, and attitudes required by the learners to perform competently. Any content or activity defined outside the realm of the identified performance problem, prerequisite knowledge or skills, or unrelated to key performances are considered outside of the program scope. Thus, a competent instructional designer will identify the scope of an instructional project based on the critical performance gap and proposed instructional solution.

Instructional goals are then created and sequenced based on program scope, for example, performance and bridging content. Instructional goals define how and when learners will engage in the instruction to become more competent in weak performance areas. These instructional goals are sequenced to help form the framework for the instructional solution.

Specific learning objectives (statements of expected outcome) and assessments (measurements of closing the performance gaps) are then created to specify how learners will engage with content and how their growth will be measured based on the instructional goals. It is critical that the instructional designer identify the type of learning outcomes (e.g., recall, apply, evaluate) required to meet the specified learning objectives. The instructional goal(s), learning objective(s), and performance outcomes(s) must all align (match up) in order to design effective instruction that will help close the identified gaps in knowledge, skills, and/or attitude.

These organizing and aligning activities often involve frequent interactions with content experts, technology specialists, and performers. Maintaining close contacts with these persons has become recognized as a crucial activity for instructional designers, as shown by the increasing interest in, and emphasis on, participatory and user-centered design (see e.g., Carr-Chellman, 2006; Carr-Chellman, Cuyar, and Breman, 1998; Koschmann, 1996).

12. Design instructional interventions *(essential)*. This is an ***essential*** competency and it includes six performance statements, all of which are essential.

   (a) Identify instructional strategies that align with instructional goals and anticipated learning outcomes *(essential)*.
   (b) Apply appropriate interaction design and interactive learning principles *(essential)*
   (c) Use appropriate message and visual design principles *(essential)*.
   (d) Apply appropriate motivational design principles *(essential)*
   (e) Accommodate social, cultural, political, and other individual factors that may influence learning *(essential)*.
   (f) Select appropriate technology and media to enhance instructional interventions, taking into account theory, research, and practical factors *(essential)*.

Instructional design competencies are at the heart of our profession. Every designer, regardless of level of experience, should gain competence in these essential performance standards. This is what we do!

One of the most basic aspects of instructional design is the selection of appropriate instructional strategies (e.g., pedagogies, activities) that align with established instructional goals and anticipated learning outcomes. This involves selecting appropriate media (technologies) and delivery systems (e.g., web-based, learning management systems) and devising activities that promote learner engagement with content and maintain their motivation to learn. However, these pedagogical and interaction decisions cannot be made without considering learner characteristics, the type of instructional context, and the nature of the content. It is one of the most creative and decision-intensive parts of the instructional design process—creating the design!

Instructional designers often develop their own mental tool box of sorts with a variety of knowledge-based (e.g., mental models, questioning scripts) and physical resources (e.g., checklists, quality assurance rubrics) that help them define appropriate instructional interventions (Eseryel, 2006; Spector, Dennen, & Koszalka, 2006). For example, they may have a developed set of questions to think through whenever presented with a proposed instructional solution, like: Do the learners have the prerequisite skills and knowledge to navigate online resources? Does the technology choice provide the type of interactivity required to engage the learner in the appropriate type of learning? Do the proposed resources provide adequate instruction and information to scaffold learning? Do the instructional strategies align with the expected learning outcomes? Are the activities motivational given the learner characteristics? Are the instructional materials designed in such a way to accommodate the social cultural, political, and other individual factors that may influence learning?

Instructional designers may have developed an expertise or series of tools that help in the application of message and visual design principles (e.g., guidelines for color, text, graphics, and multimedia) for learning products and instructional environments, in paper or digital form (Chen, 2004; Martin, 2008; Pettersson, 2007). Their mental tool box may also contain a multitude of ideas for motivational activities and resources that have proven to be effective in different environments, with different content domains, and different audiences (Keller, 1983, 1987, 2010).

Ultimately design decisions are recorded in some form of a design document (see competencies 1j, 15a, 13c) that is typically reviewed and approved by content experts and other client representatives before the instruction goes into a full development phase. This document will outline the instructional strategies, provide specifications for interactions, messages, visuals, motivational prompts, and technology and media resources.

Because instructional design is a highly dynamic, complex, and interactive activity, these design and development competencies are often difficult to separate and treat as discrete tasks. They are not completed in a step-by-step fashion in most projects, but the competent instructional designer integrates one with the other. Instructional designers must bring multiple knowledge bases together to assure that the instructional strategies developed align with the set instructional goals and anticipated learning outcomes identified in the needs assessment. Thus, instructional designers should develop practices in systemic and integrative thinking (see competency 2e) about interactive learning, message and visual design, motivation, individual factors, and technology and media choices.

Competent instructional designers select appropriate technologies, based on their features and capabilities, to support different types of learning. More often nowadays however fast-paced organizational environments often prevent designers (specially novice designers who intervene later in the process) from having much to say about selected technologies. Nonetheless, as the *learning experts* in their organizations, instructional designers should be encouraged to actively demonstrate their design and technology knowledge and seek opportunities to "educate" their clients or employer about the effectiveness of other solutions. Specifically, competent instructional designer use this knowledge to make good selections that will help to enhance instruction and engage learners in learning. With the growing demand by employers to seek instructional designers with technical expertise (e.g., elearning, mobile, and web-based instruction specialists) it is advisable that instructional designers seek additional technology skills to supplement their design competencies. Finally, it is important that instructional designers consider whether they are creating instruction for formal or informal learning environments and design interventions that are sensitive to direct and collaborative learning, social learning, online and classrooms.

The development of competency in this set of performance standards suggests that instructional designers understand the implications of the needs assessment (e.g., performance gaps; content analysis; target audience characteristics, environmental analysis) as they relate to learning (expected outcomes) and instructional theory (e.g., approaches to learning). Their understanding informs application of principles with an ultimate goal of promoting learning through quality instruction.

13. Plan noninstructional interventions *(advanced)*. This is an ***advanced*** competency and it includes three performance statements, all of which are advanced.

   (a) Identify which, if any, noninstructional interventions are appropriate (e.g., performance support, knowledge management, personnel selection, job redesign, incentive systems) *(advanced)*.

   (b) Justify why noninstructional interventions are appropriate *(advanced)*.

   (c) Create design specifications for noninstructional interventions *(advanced)*.

Not all needs assessment result in the identification of knowledge or skill gaps that can be resolved with instructional solutions. Sometimes performance issues arise because of informational or organizational issues. Performers have the knowledge, skills, and attitudes to perform but may lack information or incentives (Mager & Pipe, 1984). Instructional designers engaged in the needs assessment process have often formed a clear understanding of why performances are not meeting expectations. They may therefore be well suited to advise on plans and design some types of noninstructional solutions. For example, performers may not complete work on time because their there is a lack of incentives or a presence of dis-incentives in the work environment. Case in point, office workers receive training on new computer software that make their work process faster. They can do more work in a shorter amount of time. Project managers add to their workload, yet do not provide incentives for the workers to increase their productivity. The workers maintain the initial level of productivity, thus not meeting higher productivity levels with the new software. One solution is to provide incentives (e.g., bonuses, time off, etc.) for the additional workload. Another may be providing information to the workers about the importance of increased productivity (requiring very little changes in effort due to the new software) in an atmosphere of "increase productivity or close the plant." Instructional designers are not generally equipped to develop a new incentive system, however may advise on ideas for more effective informational message sharing (e.g., knowledge management systems, performance support systems) based on evidence from the needs assessment regarding performance and worker attitudes.

14.   Select or modify existing instructional materials *(essential)*. This is an ***essential*** competency and it includes four performance statements, two are essential and two are advanced.

   (a)   Identify and select materials that support the content analyses, proposed technologies, delivery methods, and instructional strategies *(essential)*.
   (b)   Conduct cost-benefit analyses to decide whether to use or modify existing materials *(advanced)*.
   (c)   Validate selection or modification of existing instruction *(advanced.)*
   (d)   Integrate existing instructional materials into the design *(essential)*.

All instructional designers should be able to select or modify existing instructional materials for use in resolving identified performance problems. In most situations, there is an emphasis on the modification rather than the creation of new product. An advanced instructional designer will be able to make valid selections or design modifications based on their experience. They will also have develop the practice of seeking permission to reuse or modify existing materials to avoid copyright issues. Instructional designers at all levels should also be competent at integrating value-added existing material into their new designs, again being sensitive to ownership of materials.

Recently there have been many efforts to transform existing classroom instruction into online offerings or e-learning resources. However, simply taking one set of materials designed for a particular instructional solution and then re-hosting them on a different medium or for a different instructional setting is rarely an effective practice. There are countless examples of failures trying to directly convert from classroom to online instruction or text and classroom-based instruction to digital formats (see, e.g., Koszalka & Ganesan, 2004). Competent instructional designers know that there are critical relationships between technologies, delivery methods, instructional strategies (e.g., pedagogies), learner activities, and content. Every instructional designer must know how to validate or modify existing instruction to design and create new versions for different technologies, audiences, and learning environments. Often content experts are involved in this process to assure the utility of the revised materials in the targeted setting.

One newer trend is creating re-purposable learning objects (see, e.g., Wiley, 2002). Digital libraries are available in many content domains (Harden et al., 2011) that provide instructional and learning objects that can be integrated into a variety of instructional resources and contexts. For example, many medical school courses teach and reinforce medical procedures (e.g., sutures, doctor-patient communication) in multiple courses. Learning objects that teach, for example, how to suture a wound or surgical incision are available that can be integrated into general practice of medicine courses, surgery courses, dental surgery courses and others without having to recreate the instruction for each instance (Ellaway & Masters, 2008; Hardin et al., 2011). Instructional designers who use such practices may develop additional efficiencies in creating instructional materials by reusing and modifying existing materials.

While the modification of existing materials is viewed as a basic designer skill, the ability to perform a cost-benefit analysis is not. This advanced skill is used to determine whether it is best to modify, purchase, or develop entirely new instructional material to accomplish the specific instructional goal. Budget decisions usually are made at higher levels in an organization and are most often associated with positions of responsibility. Those performing critical budget analysis are, therefore, typically the most experiences professionals. Advanced designers may be able to develop a cost-benefit analysis and advocate a stance of revising, purchasing, or developing new instructional materials based on their situation.

15. Develop instructional materials *(essential)*. This is an **essential** competency and it includes four performance statements, all of which are essential.

   (a) Develop specifications that serve as the basis for media production *(essential)*.
   (b) Produce instructional materials in a variety of delivery formats *(essential)*.
   (c) Develop materials that align with the content analyses, proposed technologies, delivery methods, and instructional strategies *(essential)*.
   (d) Collaborate with production specialists *(essential)*.

Many novice designers have positions that combine design and development tasks. This competency is perhaps the most straight forward of all 22 presented in this version of the Instructional Designer Standards, requiring the least elaboration. Nonetheless, the distinction between design and development should be reemphasized. Essentially, design activities involve systematic planning based upon data for instructional products, programs, and environments. Development is the production of those materials. Note however, that one of the first steps in development is reviewing design specifications and validating or modifying specific specification to support media production activities (e.g., video production, website design, document formatting standards). Often media specialists (e.g., video producers, programmers), working with instructional developers, will need more specificity before beginning the time intensive and detail-oriented activities involved in media production.

Instructional developers may be involved in writing instructor and participant guides (in paper or digital formats) or producing web-based instruction, or creating multimedia resources to support learning, for example. Although many designers/developers acquire competence (knowledge and skills) in a variety of delivery formats, some develop expertise in a particular medium, for example e-learning specialist, instructional video production, or distance education design specialist. Design competency accompanied with technology skills in a variety of media is challenging to find in an instructional designer given the number of packaged and proprietary technology resources. Regardless of the technologies and media skills, design competencies remain most critical to the development of successful instruction.

The development process results in instructional products or environments that integrate content, technology, delivery methods (e.g., pedagogical, technology-based), and instructional strategies that have been selected and planned in the design phase. Even though development is often seen as a technical activity, it nonetheless may involve interacting with content experts and clients as is the case in the analysis and design phases of a project. The instructional developer therefore maintains a responsibility to make sure that produced materials and environments align with the content analysis, features of chosen technologies and delivery methods, and instructional strategies laid out in the design specifications. Quality in development is driven by the advice and decisions of the instructional developer in producing from the design plan. Consequently, all designers and developers must be able to demonstrate that they can maintain product quality (e.g., instruction that will close the performance gap) and communicate effectively with all stakeholders (e.g., content experts, production specialists, media producers, clients) during the process (see competency 1).

16. **Design learning assessment (advanced).** This is an *advanced* competency and it includes three performance statements, two are essential and one is advanced.

   (a) Identify the learning processes and outcomes to be measured *(essential)*.

   (b) Construct reliable and valid methods of assessing learning and performance *(advanced)*.

   (c) Ensure that assessment is aligned with instructional goals, anticipated learning outcomes, and instructional strategies *(essential)*.

During the design and development phases instructional designers design, create, and test learning assessments. These assessment are based on the instructional goals, instructional strategies, and expected learning outcomes from the instruction. Measures must closely align (represent) the type of learning expected to occur from the provided learning activities. Competent instructional designers will carefully examine these relationships and construct methods and tools that help measure learning during and after instruction. As an advanced competency it is expected that instructional designers have been trained in methods for assessing learning and performance gains. They understand what constitutes learning in a particular situation, how to measure that learning, and how to provide constructive feedback to learners who have met learning outcome requirements or not and need remediation. This is a complex activity that requires knowledge of learning and instructional theory, at least a basic educational psychology background, and thorough understanding of how to translate instructional goals, expected learning outcomes, and designed instructional strategies into effective measures of learning. This requires advanced competencies in understanding and constructing valid and reliable measurements. During the development phase these learning assessments are fully developed with the other instructional products and tested to assure they are valid measure that produce reliable data on learning.

EVALUATION AND IMPLEMENTATION

This competency domain, Evaluation and Implementation, is one that has been introduced with this edition of the Instructional Designer Competencies. Although the previous sets of competencies included a competency on evaluation, this is the first to recognize the integral role that evaluation plays in instructional design work. The following are the competency areas associated with this domain:

- Evaluation
- Revision
- Implementation and dissemination

This competency domain recognizes the importance of evaluation in instructional design. Without some sort of evaluation, the instructional designer does not know whether or not the proposed intervention meets its objectives and is successful. Such information can then be used to determine the appropriate revisions need in instructional design plans and materials. Finally, through the evaluation work, the instructional designer can become more aware of any issues that need to be addressed with the implementation, dissemination, and diffusion of the interventions.

It should be noted, however, that two of the three competencies, along with most of the performance statements are considered to be advanced or managerial level skills. Only the one competency dealing with revisions and those performance statements involving implementation appear as essential. Nevertheless, even a novice instructional designer should become familiar with the need for evaluation and revision prior to any dissemination of instructional products and programs.

The competency and associated performance statements are outlined below, accompanied by further discussion and explanation.

17. Evaluate instructional and noninstructional interventions *(advanced)*. This is an ***advanced*** competency and it includes four performance statements, two are essential and two is advanced.

    (a) Design evaluation plans *(advanced)*.
    (b) Implement formative evaluation plans *(essential)*.
    (c) Implement summative evaluation plans *(essential)*.
    (d) Prepare and disseminate evaluation report *(advanced)*.

It should be noted that designing the evaluation and preparing the evaluation report are considered advanced skills, while the implementation of the evaluation plans is considered an essential skill. Nevertheless, it behooves every instructional designer to understand some of the basic issues surrounding evaluation. The ibstpi book on evaluator competencies may prove helpful (Russ-Eft, Bober, de la Teja, Foxon, & Koszalka, 2008).

Evaluation of organizational intervention has become more prevalent. Senior management is less willing to devote time and resources to initiatives without some data being gathered as to the effectiveness of that initiative. Planning for such evaluations comprises a critical step, and the responding instructional designers recognized that this represents an advanced instructional designer skill. Indeed, the plan for an evaluation should include many of the following components:

Evaluation rationale that describes the program and the reasons for the evaluation

- Evaluation purpose in no more than five sentences
- Stakeholders for the evaluation, along with reasons for their interest in the results
- Key evaluation questions, which should be limited in number (typically five at most)
- Evaluation design, including the kind of evaluation (such as formative or summative or performance monitoring), the evaluation model (such as responsive, empowerment, behavior objectives), the design (such as case study, ethnographic, or quasi-experimental), and the reasons for making these decisions
- Data collection, including not only the methods, but also the sampling and the instruments
- Data analysis, along with procedures to ensure the validity or trustworthiness of the instruments and the methods
- Issues and concerns, which can include constraints and the political context
- Procedures and timing in communicating and reporting progress and findings
- Management plan for the evaluation
- Budget for the evaluation

Details on each of these aspects of an evaluation can be found in Russ-Eft and Preskill (2009). Nevertheless, the present text will address three key aspects: (a) stakeholders, (b) evaluation models, and (c) issues of validity.

As noted above, one important aspect of an evaluation plan, as well as the actual evaluation, involves the stakeholders. Russ-Eft and Preskill (2009), for example, recommended that the evaluator identify three levels of stakeholders. Primary stakeholders are those who commission the evaluation and those who will be the primary users of the evaluation findings. For instructional designers, primary stakeholders may include senior management, as well as the instructional design team. Secondary stakeholders are those who are interested in the program or the evaluation. For instructional designers, these stakeholders may include middle managers affected by the intervention. Although they may not commission the evaluation, their support may be critical during the data collection. Tertiary stakeholders are those who may find value in the findings. For the instructional designer, such stakeholders may include customers or clients of the organization or possibly colleagues in other organizations.

As described by Russ-Eft and Preskill (2005), involvement and engagement of these various stakeholders in the planning and execution of the evaluation can prove critical to achieving a successful and useful evaluation. Such involvement and engagement should begin with planning the evaluation. It can continue throughout the evaluation by enlisting stakeholders in data gathering efforts and later in helping with the interpretation of the findings.

Many instructional designers are familiar with the work of Kirkpatrick (1994) and the four levels—reactions, learning, behavior, and results. Kirkpatrick introduced these concepts in the late 1950s and early 1960s (i.e., Kirkpatrick, 1959a, 1959b, 1960a, 1960b), and they seem to have taken a strangle-hold over evaluations of training, personnel development, and other organizational interventions. In the meantime, the field of program evaluation has grown and diversified, and many new and useful evaluation models have been introduced.

Evaluation models such as responsive evaluation (Stake, 1983), participatory evaluation (Cousins & Earl, 1992, 1995; Cousins & Whitmore, 1998), and utilization-focused evaluation (Patton, 2008) recognize the importance of the stakeholder in the evaluation. Furthermore, Brinkerhoff (2003, 2005a, 2005b, 2006) introduced the success case method, arguing that simply reporting the average performance was meaningless. Rather, he recommended that the evaluator examine the "successful cases," those in which the intervention proved effective, and the factors that contrasted the successful cases with those that were less successful. Such an evaluation would yield important information as to how to ensure greater success in the future.

In addition to the program evaluation models, instructional designers need to be familiar with evaluation as undertaken with rapid prototyping. Introduced by Tanik and Yeh (1989), Whitten, Bentley, and Barlow (1989), and Tripp and Richelmeyer (1990), rapid prototyping was first implemented in software development, and it has become popular in instructional design. With such rapid development, formal program evaluation may not be possible or optimal. Instead, one can use multiple formative evaluations conducted in natural settings. [See below for more discussion of formative evaluations.] Such evaluations can use unobtrusive measures, such as observation, as well as face-to-face interviews with a small number of individuals (e.g., Jones, Li, & Merrill, 1992; Tripp & Richelmeyer, 1990).

A final important aspect that needs to be considered when planning an evaluation involves the validity of the data collection and the analyses. It must be recognized that there are several forms of validity. Validity or trustworthiness can refer to the data collection process. In this case, two forms of validity are of concern: (a) internal validity and (b) external validity. Internal validity involves the quality of the data collection design, and it refers to the extent to which the data collection effort answers the question being asked. An experimental or quasi-experimental design, as well as case study or ethnographic study, can yield valid data that can be used to make decisions. In contrast, a haphazard data collection effort, whether quantitative or qualitative, may yield data, but one would not want to use those data to make any important decisions. External validity refers to the extent to which the results can be generalized. Typically, generalization relies upon the quality of the sampling effort. More about internal and external validity can be found in Russ-Eft and Preskill (2009).

In addition to internal and external validity, issues of validity need to be addressed with regard to certain data collection instruments. The Standards for Educational and Psychological Testing (American Educational Research Association, American Psychological Association, and National Council on Measurement in Education, 1999) identifies the following types of validity:

- Face validity
- Validity based on test content
- Validity based on response processes
- Validity based on internal structure
- Validity based on relations to other variables
- Validity based on consequences

Although an instructional designer need not become an expert in measurement and testing issues, it is important to be aware of some of the issues affecting the validity of any test instruments or assessments that might be used, particularly when planning the evaluation.

Regardless of the evaluation approach and the research design and methods, the evaluation implementation is likely to yield one or both of the following kinds of results: (a) formative information and/or (b) summative information. Formative results provide information that the instructional designer can use to make adjustments and improvements in the design. In contrast, summative results can lead to decisions to continue or to discontinue the program. Whichever type of information is to be gathered, the instructional designer needs to follow the evaluation plan carefully and should document any deviations that might occur during the data collection and analysis, since these deviations may affect the results.

Formative evaluations typically involve less formal evaluation designs. One approach may be to have a group of subject-matter experts review the instructional design and materials and provide feedback. Another approach may consist of observations or one-on-one interviews of users or trainees. Conducting a pilot-test within the actual setting can yield important information as to the feasibility of the design and implementation.

Summative evaluation typical involves rather formal approaches, since the decisions may lead to continuation, expansion, or elimination of the program. In some cases, the focus is upon the extent to which trainees actually use the skills on the job (or what is called transfer of training). In other cases, the evaluation is focused on the organizational impact rather than on a small group of trainees. Another focus for such evaluations can be in terms of the cost-benefit or cost-effectiveness of the instructional design and program.

A final important step in the evaluation is to provide some reporting of the results. Indeed, a critical issue for any evaluation involves dissemination and use. Furthermore, such dissemination should not be limited to the primary client; after all, those who provided data for the evaluation may also be interested in knowing what was decided. Torres, Preskill, and Piontek (2004) suggested a variety of communication and dissemination strategies to keep stakeholders informed of progress and results. These included the typical progress report and final report, and also meetings with stakeholders to plan the evaluation and review and interpret some of the findings and briefs for newsletters and other publications.

In addition to the dissemination method that might be used, the instructional designer needs to consider the content of the evaluation report, particularly in light of the potential recipients. For busy executives, a brief overview of 1 to 3 pages may be sufficient, while for those who much implement major recommendations, additional detail may be needed. For highly sophisticated and technical audiences, statistical analyses may be needed, while for others graphs and charts may suffice.

18. Revise instructional and noninstructional solutions based on data. *(essential)*. This is an ***essential*** competency and it includes three performance statements, two are essential and one is advanced.

   (a) Identify product and program revisions based on review of evaluation data *(advanced)*.
   (b) Revise the delivery process based on evaluation data *(essential)*.
   (c) Revise products and programs based on evaluation data *(essential)*.

The competency itself is rated as essential since all instructional designer should be able to revise solutions based on data and feedback that are received. The first of these performance statements, focused on reviewing the data and identifying needed revisions was rated as advanced, while the latter two, actually implementing the revisions, were rated as essential.

After having gathered the evaluation data and prepared a report of the results, the instructional designer must determine the needed revisions in the product and/or the program. Some of these may be included in the evaluation report, but others may need to be determined after a thorough review of the data.

In contrast with the concept of a formal evaluation report, rapid assessment and rapid prototyping, as mentioned above, involves evaluation followed by immediate redesign and development followed by further evaluation. These are undertaken in successive steps moving toward the final design.

Based on the evaluation results, the instructional designer may need to revise the delivery process. The data for making these changes may come from the evaluation and participant feedback or they may come from changes in professional practices or organizational policies. In this case, revisions are not being made to the content but rather to the delivery of that content. The learning environment or the delivery of the content could be web-based, face-to-face, or blended. It could include self-study materials or some sort of job aid.

Another revision that may emerge from the evaluation involves the content of the products and the programs. For example, the message itself may prove meaningless to the target audience; this may mean that the message needs to be modified or that a different target audience needs to be addressed. There may be other revisions that are needed based on the evaluation data that suggest changes in specific policies or event organizational structures. Clearly, such major revisions will need the support of executives and major stakeholders.

19. Implement, disseminate, and diffuse instructional and noninstructional interventions *(advanced)*. This is an **advanced** competency and it includes seven performance statements, three are essential and four are managerial.

    (a) Create a vision of change that aligns learning and performance goals with organizational goals *(managerial)*.

    (b) Plan for the implementation of the interventions *(advanced)*.

    (c) Plan for the dissemination of the interventions *(managerial)*.

    (d) Plan for the diffusion of the interventions *(managerial)*.

    (e) Disseminate the interventions *(advanced)*.

    (f) Monitor implementation, dissemination, and diffusion progress *(managerial)*.

    (g) Identify required modifications to implementation, dissemination, and diffusion processes *(advanced)*.

This competency is considered to be advanced, and the performance statements are rated as being managerial or advanced.

One important managerial performance involves creating a vision of change. Further that vision must align the learning and performance goals with organizational goals. Such alignment helps to ensure the linkage of any proposed intervention with the organization's strategies and goals. As shown in the work of Anderson (2009) this alignment requires dialogue and negotiation; and there needs to be involvement in various planning processes.

Planning for the implementation of the interventions is considered an advanced performance. It should be noted that implementation can also be referred to as deployment. Thus, the advanced instructional designer needs to plan the logistics of the deployment or the implementation. Such a plan must include the personnel and resources needed, and it must indicate the needed time for learners. If planning for face-to-face sessions, the plan must also discuss the location and any needed arrangements.

Planning for the dissemination of the intervention is rated as a managerial performance. Certainly, the instructional designer must work with management concerning the timing and scheduling of the intervention. Depending upon the organization's fiscal year, certain periods may pose problems for the intended audience. Furthermore, it coordination with other events and activities is critical.

Planning for implementation and dissemination are critical steps, but the savvy instructional designer also plans for diffusion of the intervention. Diffusion is not simply dissemination but rather involves activities and processes to encourage adoption and buy-in. This diffusion may include various instructional and communication strategies to support the proposed change.

The advanced instructional designer then uses the dissemination plan to actually disseminate the intervention. Such dissemination can involve working with training through one or multiple "train-the-trainer" sessions. The dissemination may involve the nitty-gritty work of ensuring that materials are in place and that needed equipment is available. It can even involve the details of shipping the materials to the correct locations. Once all of the logistical issues have been arranged, dissemination can then focus on the quality of the implementation and the progress of the learners.

The performance of monitoring implementation, dissemination, and diffusion and their progress is necessarily a managerial task. With today's technologies, the instructional designer can use learning management or course management systems to monitor learner progress and course completion. These tools will provide needed records and reports for individual and group progress. It may be necessary to develop systems for diagnosing individual and group needs and for prescribing instructional and noninstructional alternatives for individuals and groups. Such monitoring can help to ensure that the intervention is doing what was intended.

A final performance task involves using the information from the monitoring of the implementation, dissemination, and diffusion efforts to determine any needed modifications. This represents an important, but frequently overlooked step. As soon as the monitoring phase has identified some deviation or problem, the instructional designer must determine what needs to be done to move the intervention closer toward the intended implementation and outcome.

MANAGEMENT

The competencies in the management domain have been significantly modified from the 2000 ID competencies. One significant change was separating management into its own domain. This was to show the significance of these competencies to the growing profession. The field has substantially grown over the last decade and experienced instructional designer are finding themselves moving into management roles that require both competencies in instructional design practices and management activities. Management competencies are especially important because ID projects often takes place within and across dynamic organizational contexts, with distributed multidisciplinary teams, and under the influence of politics, drama, changing goals and resources, and intense competition. Instructional function or project managers are challenged with facilitating multiple projects, maintaining high quality standards across all projects, developing business cases and managing multiple budgets, developing and maintaining cross-functional teams of specialists, obtaining organizational or institutional support for instructional projects, managing partnerships, and resolving complex problems. This emerging role encompasses three competency topics.

- Applying business skills
- Managing partnerships and collaborative relationships
- Planning and managing instructional design projects.

Often, managers are held accountable for executing these competencies (see Foxon et al., 2003 ibstpi *Training Manager Competencies*); however, all professionals who engage in ID regardless of their role, sooner or later discover that the management competencies are vitally important to their own success.

Given that designing, developing, implementing, evaluation, and continuously improving instructional materials and activities is an arduous task, instructional designers and teams are required to deliver projects on time, on budget and with quality results, regardless of environmental context. It is also critical that the products, environments, and human factors of the working and implementation be carefully considered in the design and implementation of the instruction. This requires an understanding of the organization's strategic goals, culture, and organizational support and resource frameworks. The design instructional designers who manages these project must demonstrate instructional design competencies complimented by business, planning, and management skills.

The three competencies in the management domain (i.e., apply business skills to managing the instructional design function, manage partnerships and collaborative relationships, and plan and manage instructional design projects) were identified as critical to a greater degree to those instructional designers who manage projects and instructional design or training functions within an organization.

20. Apply business skills to managing the instructional design function *(managerial)*. This is a ***managerial*** competency and it includes seven performance statements, all are managerial.

   (a) Align instructional design efforts with organization's strategic plans and tactics *(managerial)*.

(b) Establish standards of excellence for the instructional design function *(managerial)*.

(c) Develop a business case to promote the critical role of the instructional design function *(managerial)*.

(d) Recruit, retain, and develop instructional design personnel *(managerial)*.

(e) Develop financial plans and controls for the instructional design function *(managerial)*.

(f) Obtain and maintain management and stakeholder support for the design function *(managerial)*.

(g) Market instructional design services and manage customer relations *(managerial)*.

Professionals who are proficient in this competency understand how ID fits within a larger organizational frame, and they operate within that frame to produce quality results. Work in organizations is assigned to various functions based on employee expertise and the work that the organization needs performed. Often the assignment of work is both political and competitive. Professionals who are successful over time recognize the importance of working in a function with other professionals who

- contribute to the organization's purpose that is defined by its mission, strategic plans, objectives, goals, and tactics
- establish and evaluate projects based on standards of excellence
- promote the function's contribution to the organization using business cases that demonstrate value
- maintain personnel, including people who are both internal and external to the organization, who can perform the functions' work.
- manage projects finances effectively
- obtain and manage project personnel by recruiting professionals with the appropriate competencies, retaining those professionals, and further developing those professionals to carry out the function's work
- promote the function's services and manage relationships with internal and external customers and stakeholders

Instructional design professionals who have this competency work with their organization's culture, structure, politics, and processes rather than against them. Those able to demonstrate these competencies are in a better position to influence the strategic thinking and actions of an organization because they can help envision how organizations align the capabilities of their personnel in response to a new strategic organizational objective. People are the most expensive resources of an organization and often the most challenging to redirect when an organization wants to change its course or increase its pace. In this regard, expert designers who are masters of these competencies can also become architects of change. Not surprising, by supporting systemic efforts they find it easier to be more successful than those who flail against the system.

Interestingly, consultants and other third party professionals use this competency and the accompanying performance statements to analyze their own tasks and reporting relationships, assuring that their own work is aligned with the larger organization. They also use the competency and performance statements to analyze potential client projects to assure that the proposed instructional design effort is positioned to be successful.

21. Manage partnerships and collaborative relationships *(managerial)*. This is a ***managerial*** competency and it includes four performance statements, one is advanced and three are managerial.

    (a) Identify stakeholders and the nature of their involvement *(advanced)*.

    (b) Build and promote effective relationships between the design team and stakeholders *(managerial)*.

    (c) Manage cross functional teams *(managerial)*.

    (d) Conduct project reviews with design team members and stakeholders *(managerial)*.

Professionals who are proficient in this competency recognize that instructional design work is accomplished with and through other people. These professionals take into account all the individuals and groups who are interested and/or involved in the work. For example, instructional design projects may include clients, content experts, supervisors and managers of content and performance areas, media specialists, evaluation specialists, learners, organization executives, and organizational groups like marketing, finance, and technology support. Note that the list of stakeholders includes managers and executives who are most likely responsible for making major decisions about instructional design efforts for the organization, including funding and resource allocation.

In addition to identifying project stakeholders, professionals who are proficient at managing partnerships and collaborative relationships also build and promote effective interactions between the design team and its stakeholders, and they manage cross functional teams. These responsibilities often are challenging because stakeholders and team members may have differing goals, points of view, values, expertise, frameworks, personal preferences, and ways of doing things. Successfully negotiating the differences among all stakeholders to move an instructional design effort forward involves the skillful use of influence, process management, and control (see standards 1 and 5).

Project reviews with design team members and stakeholders provide a way to build on the negotiations and to improve future efforts. Project reviews, sometimes called After-Action-Reviews, establish lessons learned, review progress, identify problem areas, and recognize and support positive relationships.

An instructional design function manager, for example should be able to demonstrate management competencies in activities like:

- networking with executives to get buy-in for the project and learn their expectations
- influencing, informing, and managing teams of professionals who develop content for the a training unit (i.e., the web designer, the subject expert on action planning, and the ID professional who was assigned to the project).
- monitoring and influencing interactions, activities, and performance of team members
- working with professionals from technology units to assure that technology-based and online training can be accessed to target stakeholders regardless of location
- collaborating with professionals in human resources or consultants to assure that the training materials are properly translated as required
- conducting project reviews with design team and stakeholders to review progress, establish lessons learned, identify and resolve problem, identify working relationships that are effective and those that need improvement.

These types of activities demonstrate proficiency in managing partnerships and collaborative relationships that are critical to success in today's complex and dynamic organizations.

22. Plan and manage instructional design projects (advanced). This is an ***advanced*** competency and it includes six performance statements, three are advanced and three are managerial.

   (a) Establish project scope and goals *(advanced)*.
   (b) Write proposals for instructional design projects *(advanced)*.

(c) Use a variety of planning and management tools for instructional design projects *(advanced)*.

(d) Allocate resources to support the project plan *(managerial)*.

(e) Manage multiple priorities to maintain project time line *(managerial)*.

(f) Identify and resolve project issues *(managerial)*.

The professionals who are proficient in this competency demonstrate the abilities to systematically execute instructional design function and project efforts. They set boundaries for ID projects based on the project goals and scope; then they write proposals for projects that are based on the established goals and scopes. The proposal, once accepted, becomes the framework for creating and managing instructional design project plans.

ID professionals are able to effectively use a variety of planning and management tools (e.g., Gantt chart, PERT charts, risk analysis, contingency planning) to manage projects and keep them on track. The use of these tools is viewed as applying quality project management. The insights, competencies, and tools used by the instructional design function or project manager aid in assigning required personnel, financial, and technical resources to accomplish the work. Moreover, the tools support the management of various project priorities and timelines to achieve project plan goals. Being able to effectively and continually negotiate between the performance on the project and the project plan is generally a required activity of any project manager. Often instructional design managers use rapid assessment processes to identify plan issues and resolve them swiftly by reaching agreement on the issue and potential solution with key stakeholders.

Throughout a project or within an instructional design function—from the needs assessment to the evaluation activities—instructional design professionals identify and address problems. In this way, they produce outcomes that meet the expectations for professional, ethical, cultural, quality, quantity, timeliness, and cost factors, while maintaining professional relationships. Management competencies are important to all individuals who design instruction (e.g., planning and executing daily activities, reporting progress) however are critical to those advanced and managerial instructional designers who shepherd teams and larger projects. Keeping projects within scope and relevant to the organization and all stakeholders is critical to the ultimate consumer who must close a performance gap. Competence in management skills is important in meeting these goals.

CHAPTER 4

INSTRUCTIONAL DESIGNER COMPETENCIES IN PRACTICE

INTRODUCTION

There are at least four general groups of professionals who use the instructional designer (ID) competencies in their work:

- Instructional design practitioners
- Instructional design (or training) managers and administrators
- Instructional design-oriented academics
- Organizations that offer instructional design-related professional development

Each of these types of users are likely to approach the application of the Instructional Designer competencies with differing needs, and consequently use them in a unique manner. Instructional design practitioners may use them as a benchmark to guide their professional development while ID (or training) managers and administrators may use them for human resources functions like recruiting and personnel evaluation. Academics may use them for research and curriculum planning purposes. Professional associations may use them to guide the design of professional development programs they offer or as guidelines to help their audience select appropriate workshops and experiences that will support their professional development needs.

Instructional Designer Competencies: The Standards, Fourth Edition, pp. 69–80
Copyright © 2013 by Information Age Publishing

The instructional designer competencies do more than describe instructional designer skills, knowledge, and attitudes. They describe instructional designer job position requirements and provide a common language for a field that transcends cultural boundaries. In essence, they define the instructional design profession. Competency models provide guidance for those entering the field as well as for veterans seeking opportunities to update their knowledge and improve their performance value. The competencies can also suggest parameters for specialty areas and provide direction for improving an instructional design organization.

This chapter will examine the major uses of the ID competencies by these four groups of professionals. Each section will provide a description of the role followed by a discussion of the implications of these competencies for the practitioner, a description of how the ID competencies relate to the work of professional, and examples of current issues where the competencies may help. Each section will end with a short *case in point* section suggesting specific areas where the ID competencies will support each type of user given current and expected future trends in our field. The chapter ends with a brief summary about the uses and underlying assumptions about the uses of these competencies in multiple contexts.

INSTRUCTIONAL DESIGNER COMPETENCY UTILITY

Competency Use by Instructional Design Professionals

Planning for individual professional development. Consumers of instructional design services are becoming increasingly sophisticated and have higher performance expectations for designers. Consequently, those in the design field are forced to upgrade their competencies to remain competitive. The 2012 ID competencies provide direction in this process, thereby supporting the advancement of individual careers and adding value to the organizations they serve. In essence, the competencies and performance statements can serve as robust criteria for professional development planning. This is possible given their established content validity and that fact that they highlight how the profession is evolving. The ID competencies define those skills now expected in the marketplace. They also provide a reference point for the coming decade and as such provide a framework for ongoing professional development efforts. They provide designers a means of comparing their own competencies and performance capabilities against an external benchmark established by professional peer groups.

The questions provided in Table 4.1 provide a guide for professional development planning. These questions can be used to structure self-assessment of one's competencies and help plan ways (e.g., professional development, practice, new experiences) of filling gaps. Such self-assessments can be conducted in addition to routine performance assessments, in preparation for advanced graduate study, or during the selection of professional development workshops.

Table 4.1. Questions for Analyzing ID Professional Development Needs

Question
Do I require this competency or capability to perform my current job assignments?
Do I require this competency or capability for future work assignments or promotional opportunities?
Is this competency or performance statement one for which I have a particular talent or interest?
Do I have this competency or performance capability?
Can I perform at the appropriate level of proficiency?
If needed, can I acquire the competency or capability in a professional development program?

Novice and experienced designers may use this self-assessment in different ways. Novices might focus on the particular competencies required for specific upcoming projects when preparing for a specific position for which they aspire. Novices and experienced designers alike might also use this self-assessment process to enhance their overall employability when changing or seeking new positions.

Experienced designers, especially those who received formal training some time ago, typically have other concerns. This self-assessment process may be particularly important when they need to update their skill sets. They may be deficient in performance analysis techniques, new technologies, or some other key design tasks, for example. The competencies and performance statements may introduce to experienced designers new terms and concepts currently used in the field. The experienced designer may wish to focus upon those competencies that help him or her excel in a specialty area of the design process, like front-end analysis, evaluation, or project management. Experienced designers may also want to review *ibstpi's evaluator and training manager* competency sets, as they provide more specific competency sets. Acquisition of these competencies can facilitate the transition from a generalist designer role to that of a specialist, from a developer of learning solutions to an organizational strategist. These are some specific ways in which the competencies can be used as a basis for in-depth professional development and acquiring advanced and management levels of designer expertise.

Case in point. Areas in professional development that continue to emerge and often require new competency development include globalization of instruction, retraining of the workforce based on economic recession and declines in industry, rapid development of new industries, growth of e-learning and distance education, and spread of mobile technologies. Although a foundation of strong instructional design competencies prepares instructional designers for most situations, specialized skills and knowledge will be helpful in creating instruction that meets these types of needs. The ID competencies do not specify specific technology or environmental issues that all instructional designers should possess, however, this updated version suggests that preparedness for new technologies, environments, audiences, and practice models are critical to successful work in this field. The point is to develop an understanding of these trends and then determine the best ways to apply foundational design principles in instructional solutions. This by no means is suggesting that instructional designers become experts in different cultures or skilled in programming using a variety of tools. It suggests that instructional designers need to update their knowledge of these trends so that they can ask better questions, work more effectively with subject matter experts and technicians, create learning solutions that are appropriate for their given situation, and become more effective at demonstrating the impact of these solutions in the organizations they serve.

COMPETENCY USE BY INSTRUCTIONAL DESIGN (OR TRAINING) MANAGERS AND ADMINISTRATORS

Instructional design (or training) managers are another group acutely concerned with designer competence, both personally and in their instructional designer staff. Competency is important to personnel and project management and often critical in building Instructional design or training functions that align with the organization at large.

Managing Human Resources Function. The competencies can be useful for managers and administrators as they engage in a variety of human resources activities. First, these competencies can serve as guidelines for the formation or revision of job descriptions and career development models. Used in this way the competencies can help designers and project managers alike. Designers can see what skills are required for a particular position and then determine if they are likely to be promoted through the various levels once on the job. Managers can similarly use them as aids in the recruitment and hiring of new designers to help insure that prospective employees have those competencies required for a given position. The 2012 competencies are particularly useful for these purposes since they distinguish between those competencies needed by novice, experienced, and managerial instructional design professionals. Moreover, they highlight those specific skills required for more focused design roles such as analyst or project manager.

Similarly, the competencies can also be used as a basis for selecting external consultants or vendors. This is increasingly important with the heavy reliance upon outsourcing and the corresponding proliferation of freelance instructional designers. The process for using the competencies for vendor selection parallels their use with permanent employees.

Managers can also use the competencies to offer specific job performance feedback to practicing designers. The competencies can form the basis of performance appraisal, mentoring, and coaching programs. They offer a framework for planning the further development of individuals, as well as intact design teams. This form of assessment provides the manager with insight into department strengths and weaknesses. It may lead to identifying needs for further professional development, or perhaps for hiring additional staff or outsourcing of particular design roles. This identification is particularly important when an organization begins to transition from a training development mindset into a performance improvement consulting approach. Such radical transformations in process and mindset demand systematic examination of the organization's composite skill sets and planning for upgrading in those newly required competencies.

Managing Projects and Teams. Today much of the work in a complex training operation is team-based. The teams are typically cross-functions, often nowadays international and distributed, and it is important for the design capabilities to be fully covered within these teams. In addition, it is increasingly the case that these teams are virtual, which puts a premium on communication and technology skills as well as a common language of design. The ID competencies can guide project managers when they form these project teams. They can be used to more precisely select designers who possess specific require skill sets. Team members can be selected by referring to the competencies to insure the team has the range of competencies needed for projects. Using the competences in this manner will allow an organization to custom build project teams capable of performing successfully. They can also serve as guidelines for directing the team and pointing to the need for additional team resources.

Benchmarking. Benchmarking is now a standard activity in both small and large organizations. The new ID competencies can play a role in this process as well. Managers wishing to benchmark their design group against leaders in the field can use the competencies as the standard of excellence by which they can compare themselves to similar organization. When used in this way the competencies allow an organization to verify its level of excellence by providing evidence that it complies with this internationally vetted and validated set of standards.

Educating Management. In many organizations, leaders and managers are not familiar with instructional systems design, or the degree of knowledge, skills, attitudes, and experience required to design and implement effective instructional design projects. An important part of a manager's role then is to educate upper management. The ID competencies can be used as an external authority in this process. Often such explanations are imperative if a department is to receive the resources required to be successful. For example, a design team may be capable of designing instruction that produces the intended learning outcomes, but display little capability to conduct an impact evaluation that assesses the effect of a particular intervention on the organization. The manager in this scenario can use the competencies as an external standard to define the complexities of the task to higher-level management and thus demonstrate the need for additional resources for the design team.

Managers may use the questions in Table 4.2 as a guide for addressing the various personnel and project management issues that can be influenced by these competencies.

Table 4.2. Questions for Persons Managing ID Functions

Question
Do the job descriptions of members in the current ID department or team reflect the range of required competencies?
Do current employees demonstrate design competence required for their particular job?
Do the team members have the competencies required for an upcoming project?
Does the prospective employee have the specific skills required for the position?
Do the competencies of the prospective employee complement those of the department or team?
Has the prospective consultant or vendor provided evidence of competence in the specific needed areas?
What is the mix of competencies of our instructional design (or training) staff; overall, what are our strengths and weaknesses)?
Is it clear to others within and outside of the organization the range of competence and capabilities of the department or team?
Are my competencies as an instructional design manager or administrator current?

Case in point. Areas in instructional design function management that continue to emerge and often require new competency development include changes in Human Resources (Instructional Design or Training) Department terminology and functions (e.g., talent management; outsourcing specialized skills; transitioning training from classroom to e-learning or technology-supported learning; growth in cross-functional and international teams dedicated to human performance issues; and evidence-based funding of internal projects). Instructional design (training) function managers can use the ID competencies to develop their own knowledge of the ID process and to create instructional design teams that have the skills and knowledge to successfully solve human performance issues in their organization. The ID managers and administrators can use the ID competencies to evaluate instructional designers, create project management plans based on competency sets of available employees, recruit new employees or consultants that will provide specialized skills sets for emerging projects, or identify training needs for current instructional designers. They can also be used both to benchmark team strengths and justify to upper management training, hiring, and outsourcing efforts.

COMPETENCY USE BY INSTRUCTIONAL DESIGN-ORIENTED ACADEMICS

The ibstpi instructional designer competencies can be useful for those who prepare future instructional designers and study their professional development. Many colleges and universities include programs or portions of programs devoted to instructional design work. Such instructional design concepts typically appear in graduate programs focused on instructional design, educational technology, and human resource development. The ID competencies can be used to develop and update the curricula, support accreditation of instructional design programs, assess student performance, and establish research agendas.

Developing and updating curricula. Graduate programs that include an instructional design emphasis are often shaped based on faculty understanding of the skills needed in the workplace, literature in the field, and their own capabilities and vision of the field. The new ibstpi ID competencies serve as a useful tool to faculty by identifying, vetting, and documenting the competencies currently demanded in the global workplace. As such, these competencies service as a means of articulation between universities and the consumers of ID services.

The ID competency domains (e.g., professional foundations, planning and analysis, design and development, evaluation and implementation, and management) can serve as an organizing framework for course development. For example, *professional foundations* domain can provide the basis for an introductory course or courses. The *planning and analysis* and *design and development* domains may help to focus more advanced courses. The *Evaluation And Implementation* domain may also be included in more advanced courses or may serve to design specialization courses. Finally, the *Management* domain competencies provide course content ideas for advanced students planning to enter large, complex organizations, as project or instructional design function leaders.

In addition to suggesting ideas for course development, the competencies and performance statements can serve as the basis for review and revision of existing curricula, which happens in an ongoing manner in academia. Faculty can use the competencies to determine the program's relevance, completeness, and depth. For the periodic program reviews, the domains, competencies, and performance statements can be used to develop a program's self-study materials.

Moving to the course level, these competencies can serve as course objectives that inform both content and practice activities. Faculty may also use the ibstpi ID competencies as a means of student assessment, whether in the form of some sort of exam or in the development of a portfolio. The ID competencies also provide a source of self-assessment to students who can reflect on their learning experiences and comfort in practicing instructional design.

Finally, the ibstpi ID competencies can be used by faculty to guide and mentor students who may be interested in careers focused on instructional design. Both faculty and students can use the competencies as a guide to determine which courses and experiences will enable the student to develop the needed competencies.

Table 4.3 displays questions for those teaching, developing, or revising academic programs in instructional design.

Accrediting or assessing ID programs. Most academic programs undergo periodic reviews that are undertaken by internal and external accrediting or assessment bodies. Typically, the particular program must submit a self-study document reviewing the curriculum, the faculty, and the students. Although the internal and external bodies have guidelines and questions that program must address, it is typically left to the program to describe specific criteria that address their particular mission. Since the criteria that are used must be valid and reflective of the field, the ibstpi ID competencies offer programs the needed standards for this program self-study document. Thus, the ID competencies can assist the faculty in analyzing and documenting the program, assessing the program content, measuring student progress, and serve as a basis for benchmarking best ID practices.

Assessing student performance. In addition to program and course use, the ibstpi ID competencies can be used to assess student performance and progress. Several of the competencies and performance statements are considered *essential*, and therefore, students should be expected to become familiar with those competencies and should be able to demonstrate their own level of competence. Assessing student performance and progress can be undertaken using tests, demonstrations, projects, practicum experiences, and internships. Portfolios of instructional analysis,

Table 4.3. Questions for University Faculty Reviewing Instructional Design Program Curricula

Question
To what extent does the curriculum address each of the competency domain areas?
To what extent does the curriculum content address (e.g., present, provide practice) each of the competencies and performance statements?
Are there adequate practice activities to address all of the competencies and performance standards?
Are students introduced to the ibstpi instructional designer competencies as a way to track their own development?
How effectively are the competencies used to advise students who are interested in preparing for generalist and specialty careers in instructional design?
How effectively are the competencies used to guide the placement of, and assessment of, students in relevant internships and work-study programs?
To what extent does the curriculum address the professional development needs of graduate students currently working as instructional designers?
How many additional faculty are needed to increase the number and content of courses required to adequately address the range of competencies needed in the current market?

design, development, evaluation, and implementation projects are another approach to assessing student competencies. Students can use the ibstpi ID competencies to describe how their portfolio demonstrates their competence in instructional design. Faculty can use the competency and performance statements to create rubrics to evaluate student portfolios and assess their progress.

Establishing research agendas. University faculty members are often expected to undertake original research agendas. Much of that work focuses on individual interests and expertise. Nevertheless, the ibstpi ID competencies can provide some direction for future research plans. These competencies describe the scope and emphasis of current instructional design practices and they provide a comprehensive listing of topics important to practitioners. Research focused on any of these topics can be directed to the concerns and needs of both the academic and practitioner communities.

Specific research questions suggested by the ibstpi ID competencies may include the following:

- To what extent are emerging technologies changing the practice of instructional design and changing or reprioritizing the competencies?

- To what extent are evolving views of human learning changing the practices of instructional design?

- To what extent is globalization of instruction changing the practices of instructional design?
- What is the relationship, if any, between organization size and culture on the competency profiles of instructional designers?
- To what extent do persons in related fields (such as organizational development or human resource development) demonstrate instructional design competence?

Case in point. Areas in academe that continue to emerge and often require new competency development include changes in theory, practice, and terminology (e.g., learning theories, instructional design theories), major shifts in academe from classroom to e-learning, technology-supported instruction, and distance education; growth in numbers of international students; and changes in accreditation processes. The Instructional Designer competency set is useful to faculty in maintaining relevant and applicable curriculum for students preparing for careers in instructional design. Emergence of new and improved social networking technologies, mobile technologies, thinking and learning models, rapid prototyping approaches to development, and entrepreneurial emphasis often shape the ways higher education delivers curriculum and engages learners in the content of the curriculum. The uniqueness of the academic environment is that it provides a safe environment in which students can explore and experiment with these new trends in preparation for professional positions that require competent practitioners. Although the ID competencies and performance statements do not enter into such specificity, they do suggest foundational knowledge and skills of a competent instructional designer. It is up to faculty to engage students in and with these different trends while helping them develop the foundational competencies critical to their success in the profession.

COMPETENCY USE BY ORGANIZATIONS THAT OFFER INSTRUCTIONAL DESIGN-RELATED PROFESSIONAL DEVELOPMENT

Various organizations may also make use of ibstpi ID competencies. One critical area of concern for such organizations focuses on the development and professional improvement of its members. In such cases, associations can use the ibstpi ID competencies as a guide to identify areas and topics for professional development workshops for its members. Some of the issues identified in the section above on professional development specialists and consultants may be relevant for associations as they undertake development of their members.

Closely tied to such professional development concerns is the focus of some organizations on *certification*. Certification consists of a designation that a particular individual is qualified to perform a certain job. It means that the certifying body assures that the individual demonstrates the knowledge skills, abilities, and attitudes to a specified standards. Such certification can be distinguished from being *credentialed, degreed, accredited,* or *licensed*.

Less formal than professional development workshops and certification efforts, associations may view the ibstpi ID competencies as topics of concern for their members. Thus, they may want to provide webinars or short sessions at conferences devoted to some of the domains or competencies.

In summary, organizations that utilize the ibstpi ID competencies in formal certification or in less formal development venues, should consider both the organization and the individual member benefits. Some of the benefits include:

- Illustrating the organization's commitment to high quality and high performance of its members
- Indicating the organization's focus on member satisfaction and development
- Suggesting that the organization recognizes the importance of professional growth and development of its members

At the same time, members would see the following personal benefits:

- Demonstrating a level of competence superior to others in the field
- Building personal confidence
- Strengthening career advancement opportunities

CONCLUSIONS

A variety of uses for the ID competencies have been suggested in this chapter. They can be used by design practitioners and consultants, design managers, instructional design-oriented academics, and professional associations. This is not an exhaustive list, however, prospective students for example can use these competencies as a basis for evaluating the utility of a given academic programs. There are likely other applications of these competencies as well.

There is an underlying assumption that the use of the ID competencies should transcend geographic setting, organizations, and to some extent time. This is because of the generic characteristic of the competencies and performance statements, their international vetting, and the ability for particular users to customize their use without concomitant lost of integrity. Still the competencies provide a common design language as well as a common set of skills, knowledge, and attitudes upon which competence is defined for instructional designers worldwide. This allows them to be transported to many settings.

Even though the competencies as a whole are comprehensive, they can also be viewed from the perspective of those in various design specialty fields. This orientation will be discussed in Chapter 5.

CHAPTER 5

THE COMPETENCIES AND ID SPECIALIZATIONS

INTRODUCTION

A competent and experienced instructional designer can demonstrate the skills associated with the systematic design process and, therefore, is capable of managing a design project from needs assessment throughout the design, development, implementation, and evaluation phases. In many organizations, instructional designers continue to perform all the phases of a design project, but there is an increasing trend towards specialization, especially in large organizations or in situations where an instructional project or part of a project is outsourced to specialists.

A number of factors contributed to this change. First, the profession itself is becoming more complex and sophisticated, which in turn leads to specialization. As an example, the transition from a training focus to a performance improvement consulting approach highlights the necessity for strong human performance analysis skills, and in many organizations this has led to a specialization in analysis. Second, management's emphasis on accountability and evidence of return on the investment has resulted in a greater emphasis on evaluation and measurement. Third, the increasing professionalization and specialization has led to a need for those who can manage the complexities of this group of professionals. Fourth, the shift from designing for a classroom instructor to designing technology-based instruction has led to the emergence of multimedia

Instructional Designer Competencies: The Standards, Fourth Edition, pp. 81–112
Copyright © 2013 by Information Age Publishing

designers and designers of distance education and learning, a role that is rapidly evolving into the e-learning specialist.

The increased use of ID specialists can also be attributed to the globalization of organizations, which has led to an increase in the number and diversity of people to be trained and developed. In some organizations, it is not unusual for tens of thousands of people located in more than a dozen countries to require the similar training. In such cases, a single designer cannot handle a project of this size, and a design team is established. The team typically includes content experts from technical groups in the organization, as well as specialists from other fields, such as human resource development, organization development, information technology, marketing, and communications. While many teams continue to use generalist instructional designers, there is often a group of instructional designers on the team who specialize in certain aspects of the design process such as front-end analysis, technology design and integration, and evaluation.

Simultaneously, there is a trend in many large organizations to downsize and build a leaner workforce. Consequently, much of the instructional design work is now being outsourced. This leads to the use of an internal designer specializing in project management. Often the project managers will manage several projects simultaneously.

THE NATURE OF ID SPECIALIZATION

There are a number of established or emerging specialist roles in the field of instructional design. Four roles—ID specialist, analyst/evaluator, ID manager, and e-learning/instructional technology specialists—have evolved and are common in many settings. The specialists in each role have unique skill sets:

- *ID Specialists*—possessing the competencies to fulfill all roles and specializations in the design, development and implementation of an instructional solutions and usually has a preferred role in designing learning experiences and environments.
- *Analyst/Evaluator*—possessing advanced competencies to undertake performance analysis, training needs assessment, and various forms of assessment and evaluation.
- *ID Manager*—possessing advanced competencies to manage an instructional design function within an organization and manage internal and external designers and other specialists working on

one or several projects; ID managers should also possess ID competencies.
- *e-Learning/Instructional Technology Specialist*—possessing the competencies to design and develop multimedia and online learning processes and products

Although these are not the only specialist roles in the field, they are the most widely recognizable ones. In some organizations, these roles may be combined or separated depending upon project and organizational idiosyncrasies. Nevertheless, it is far more likely that several ID specialists will be found working together in large rather than small organizations. Many specialists may also be independent consultants who specialize in chosen areas of work, for example, evaluators primarily supporting program evaluation, e-learning specialists primarily engage in development of technology-based or supported instruction.

Specialists have generally mastered most of the design competencies, however have a special interest and highly developed competencies in one area of instructional design (e.g., distance education, conducting front end analysis, program evaluation). The most critical competencies required by each of the major specialist roles are summarized in Table 5.1.

The designations in the Table 5.1. were made and validated by business, government, education, and academic practitioners and scholars who are themselves generalist and specialist from around the world. Some competencies are labeled "primary" (designated by an upper case "P"), and some are labeled "supporting" (designated by a lower case "s").

Primary competencies are most critical to the specialization. For example, as analyst or evaluator requires advanced and in-depth skills in *using appropriate analysis techniques*, *constructing valid and reliable learner assessment*, and *preparing evaluation reports*. The supporting competencies, while necessary, are usually not as central to the performance of the role in most job situations. The mature specialist will be able to demonstrate both the primary and supporting competencies.

In addition, design specialists typically have in-depth knowledge of all of the essential design skills, as well as an understanding of the other specializations. They are aware of the relationships among the various roles and have an appreciation for cross-specialization. The same pattern follows for the other specialization.

Within each of the four roles, the various required skills have been grouped into the five competency domains—professional foundations, planning and analysis, design and development, evaluation and implementation, and management. A discussion of each role follows the Table 5.1.

Table 5.1.   Specialist Roles: Primary and Supporting Competencies

Domains, Competencies, & Performance Statements	ID Specialist	ID Manager	Analyst/ Evaluator	e-learning Specialist
Professional Foundations				
1. Communicate effectively in visual, oral and written form.				
a) Write and edit messages that are clear, concise, and grammatically correct	P	P	P	P
b) Deliver presentations that effectively engage audiences and communicate clear messages		P	P	
c) Use active listening skills	P	P	P	P
d) Present written and oral messages that take into account the type of information being delivered and the diverse backgrounds, roles, and varied responsibilities of the audience	P		P	P
e) Facilitate meetings effectively		P	P	
f) Use effective collaboration and consensus-building skills	s	P		s
g) Use effective negotiation and conflict resolution skills	s	P		s
h) Use effective questioning techniques	P	s	P	P
i) Solicit, accept, and provide constructive feedback	P	P	P	P
j) Disseminate status, summary, or action-oriented reports		P	P	
2. Apply research and theory to the discipline of instructional design.				
a) Promote how instructional design research, theory, and practice literature may affect design practices in a given situation	s			s
b) Explain key concepts and principles related to instructional design	s	P		s
c) Apply results of instructional design research, theory, and practice	s			s
d) Apply concepts, techniques, and theories of other disciplines to learning and performance improvement	s			P
e) Apply systems thinking to instructional design and performance improvement projects	P	P		P

(*Table continues on next page*)

Table 5.1. Continued

Domains, Competencies, & Performance Statements	ID Specialist	ID Manager	Analyst/ Evaluator	e-learning Specialist
Professional Foundations				
3. Update and improve knowledge, skills, and attitudes pertaining to the instructional design process and related fields.				
a) Participate in professional development activities				
b) Establish and maintain contacts with other professionals	s		s	s
c) Acquire and apply new technology skills in instructional design practice	s			P
d) Document and disseminate work as a foundation for future efforts, publications, or professional presentations				
4. Apply data collection and analysis skills in instructional design projects.				
a) Identify the data to be collected	s		P	s
b) Use a variety of data collection tools and procedures	s		P	s
c) Apply appropriate data collection methodologies to needs assessment and evaluation	s		P	s
d) Use appropriate quantitative and/or qualitative analysis procedures in needs assessment and evaluation	s		P	s
5. Identify and respond to ethical, legal, and political implications of design in the workplace.				
a) Identify ethical, legal, and political dimensions of instructional design practice and instructional products		s		
b) Plan for and respond to ethical, legal, and political consequences of design decisions		s		
c) Recognize and respect the intellectual property rights of others	P	s		P
d) Adhere to regulatory guidelines and organizational policies	s	s		s
e) Comply with organizational and professional codes of ethics				

(Table continues on next page)

Table 5.1. **Continued**

Domains, Competencies, & Performance Statements	ID Specialist	ID Manager	Analyst/ Evaluator	e-learning Specialist
Planning and Analysis				
6. Conduct a needs assessment in order to recommend appropriate design solutions and strategies.				
a) Identify varying perceptions of need among stakeholders and the implications of those perceptions			P	
b) Describe the nature of a learning or performance problem	P		s	P
c) Determine the root causes of identified discrepancies	P		s	P
d) Synthesize findings to identify and recommend potential instructional and noninstructional solutions	P		P	P
e) Estimate costs and benefits of possible solutions	s		P	s
f) Prepare and disseminate a needs assessment report			P	
7. Identify and describe target population and environmental characteristics.				
a) Determine characteristics of the target population that may impact the design and delivery of instruction	s		s	s
b) Determine characteristics of physical, social, political, and cultural environment that may influence learning, attitudes, and performance	s		s	s
c) Identify the infrastructure that is available to support the design and delivery of instruction	s			P
d) Determine the extent to which organizational mission, philosophy, and values may impact the design and delivery of instruction	s		s	s
e) Analyze, evaluate, and use learner profile data and environmental characteristics to design instruction	P		P	P
8. Select and use analysis techniques for determining instructional content.				
a) Identify the scope of required content in accordance with needs assessment findings	P			P

(Table continues on next page)

Table 5.1. Continued

Domains, Competencies, & Performance Statements	ID Specialist	ID Manager	Analyst/ Evaluator	e-learning Specialist
Planning and Analysis				
b) Elicit, synthesize, and validate content from subject matter experts	P		P	P
c) Analyze existing instructional products to determine adequacy or inadequacy of content, instruction, and learning	P			P
d) Determine the breadth and depth of intended content coverage given instructional constraints	s			s
e) Determine subordinate and prerequisite skills and knowledge	s			s
f) Use appropriate techniques to analyze various types and sources of content			P	
9. Analyze the characteristics of existing and emerging technologies and their potential use.				
a) Describe the capabilities of existing and emerging technologies required to enhance the impact of instruction	s			P
b) Evaluate the capacity of given instructional and learning environments to support selected technologies	P		P	P
c) Assess the benefits and limitations of existing and emerging technologies	s		s	P
Design and Development				
10. Use an instructional design and development process appropriate for a given project.				
a) Select or create an instructional design process based the nature of the project	s	P		s
b) Modify the instructional design process as project parameters change	P	P		P
c) Describe a rationale for the selected, created or modified instructional design process	s	P		s
11. Organize instructional programs and/or products to be designed, developed, and evaluated.				
a) Determine the overall scope of instructional programs and/or products	P	P		P
b) Identify and sequence instructional goals	P			P

(Table continues on next page)

Table 5.1.   Continued

Domains, Competencies, & Performance Statements	ID Specialist	ID Manager	Analyst/ Evaluator	e-learning Specialist
Design and Development				
c) Specify and sequence the anticipated learning and performance outcomes	P			P
12. Design instructional interventions.				
a) Identify instructional strategies that align with instructional goals and anticipated learning outcomes	P			P
b) Apply appropriate interaction design and interactive learning principles	P			P
c) Use appropriate message and visual design principles	P			P
d) Apply appropriate motivational design principles	s			s
e) Accommodate social, cultural, political, and other individual factors that may influence learning	s			s
f) Select appropriate technology and media to enhance instructional interventions, taking into account theory, research, and practical factors	s			P
13. Plan noninstructional interventions.				
a) Identify which, if any, noninstructional interventions are appropriate (e.g., performance support, knowledge management, personnel selection, job redesign, incentive systems)	s	P		s
b) Justify why noninstructional interventions are appropriate	s	P		s
c) Create design specifications for noninstructional interventions	P	s		P
14. Select or modify existing instructional materials.				
a) Identify and select materials that support the content analyses, proposed technologies, delivery methods, and instructional strategies	P			P
b) Conduct cost-benefit analyses to decide whether to use or modify existing materials		P	P	
c) Validate selection or modification of existing instruction	s			s

(Table continues on next page)

Table 5.1. Continued

Domains, Competencies, & Performance Statements	ID Specialist	ID Manager	Analyst/ Evaluator	e-learning Specialist
Design and Development				
d) Integrate existing instructional materials into the design	P			P
15. Develop instructional materials.				
a) Develop specifications that serve as the basis for media production	P			P
b) Produce instructional materials in a variety of delivery formats	P			P
c) Develop materials that align with the content analyses, proposed technologies, delivery methods, and instructional strategies	P			P
d) Collaborate with production specialists	S			S
16. Design learning assessment.				
a) Identify the learning processes and outcomes to be measured	P		P	P
b) Construct reliable and valid methods of assessing learning and performance			P	
c) Ensure that assessment is aligned with instructional goals, anticipated learning outcomes, and instructional strategies	P		P	P
Evaluation and Implementation				
17. Evaluate instructional and noninstructional interventions.				
a) Design evaluation plans	S		P	S
b) Implement formative evaluation plans	P		P	P
c) Implement summative evaluation plans	S			S
d) Prepare and disseminate evaluation report			P	
18. Revise instructional and noninstructional solutions based on data.				
a) Identify product and program revisions based on review of evaluation data	P		P	P
b) Revise the delivery process based on evaluation data	P			P
c) Revise products and programs based on evaluation data	P			P

(Table continues on next page)

Table 5.1. Continued

Domains, Competencies, & Performance Statements	ID Specialist	ID Manager	Analyst/ Evaluator	e-learning Specialist
Evaluation and Implementation				
19. Implement, disseminate, and diffuse instructional and noninstructional interventions.				
a) Create a vision of change that aligns learning and performance goals with organizational goals	s	P		s
b) Plan for the implementation of the interventions		P		
c) Plan for the dissemination of the interventions		s		
d) Plan for the diffusion of the interventions		s		
e) Disseminate the interventions				
f) Monitor implementation, dissemination, and diffusion progress		P		
g) Identify required modifications to implementation, dissemination, and diffusion processes	s			s
Management				
20. Apply business skills to managing the instructional design function.				
a) Align instructional design efforts with organization's strategic plans and tactics		P	s	
b) Establish standards of excellence for the instructional design function		P		
c) Develop a business case to promote the critical role of the instructional design function		P		
d) Recruit, retain, and develop instructional design personnel		P		
e) Develop financial plans and controls for the instructional design function		P		
f) Obtain and maintain management and stakeholder support for the design function		P		
g) Market instructional design services and manage customer relations		P		

(Table continues on next page)

Table 5.1. **Continued**

Domains, Competencies, & Performance Statements	ID Specialist	ID Manager	Analyst/ Evaluator	e-learning Specialist
Management				
21. Manage partnerships and collaborative relationships.				
a) Identify stakeholders and the nature of their involvement		P	P	
b) Build and promote effective relationships between the design team and stakeholders	s	P		s
c) Manage cross functional teams		P		
d) Conduct project reviews with design team members and stakeholders	s	P	s	s
22. Plan and manage instructional design projects.				
a) Establish project scope and goals	s	P		s
b) Write proposals for instructional design projects	s	s	s	s
c) Use a variety of planning and management tools for instructional design projects		P		
d) Allocate resources to support the project plan		P		
e) Manage multiple priorities to maintain project time line		P		
f) Identify and resolve project issues		P		

THE INSTRUCTIONAL DESIGNER SPECIALIST

Although all practicing IDs are generally competent in the design standards, ID specialists are generally experienced, senior designers whose interests and focus are specifically on design and learning integrity of instructional products. Their expertise is in designing instructional solutions aimed as closing identified knowledge, skill, or attitude gaps in performance. ID specialists are well prepared to design instructional solutions that can operate within a variety of delivery mechanisms (e.g., face-to-face, online, and blended learning environments). As indicated in Table 5.1, in the 2012 ID Competencies there are 34 primary performance statements and 39 secondary performance across 21 competencies clustered in 5 general domains that define the ID specialist. Together, these competencies reflect the complexity of the instructional designer specialist's role.

The ID specialist is responsible for the design integrity of the instructional solution and accomplish most tasks in collaboration with subject matter experts, performance analysts, technicians, evaluators, and others. ID specialists also play a major role in working with clients to define instructional needs and translate those needs into well designed instructional solutions.

ID specialists generally begin their career as an entry-level instructional designer actively developing experiences (and competencies) in design, development, implementation, and evaluation of instructional solutions. Through these experiences, additional professional development activities, and ongoing reflection on instructional sciences, theories, and practices ID specialists develop great interests in design and in-depth competencies of a design specialist.

Given the ID specialist's primary and secondary duties throughout the instructional design process, it is not surprising to see that they develop strong instructional design knowledge, skills, and attitudes throughout the five domains of the instructional designer competencies set including:

- *Professional Foundations*, with a primary emphasis on communications skills, systems thinking, and secondary emphasis on applying research and theory, continually improving competencies on the ID process, applying data collection and analysis skills, responding to ethical, legal, and political implications in the workplace
- *Planning and Analysis*, with primary emphasis on identifying learner and environmental characteristics and using analysis techniques to determine instructional content
- *Design and Development*, with primary emphasis using appropriate design processes, organizing instructional programs, designing

instructional and noninstructional interventions, developing or modifying instructional products and assessment, with secondary emphasis on planning noninstructional interventions

- *Evaluation and Implementation*, with primary emphasis revising instructional interventions based on evaluation data, with secondary emphasis on implementing and evaluating instruction.

- *Management*, with a secondary emphasis on managing partnerships and collaborative relationships with other team members and planning instructional design projects

Professional Foundations

The most critical competency in this domain for ID specialists is to communicate effectively in visual, oral, and written form. The competencies that are secondary to the ID specialist in this domain include: applying research and theory to the discipline of ID, updating and improving knowledge, skills, and attitudes pertaining to the instructional design process and related fields, and applying data collection and analysis skills in instructional design projects.

Certainly, ID specialists need to have well developed writing and presentation skills given their tasks of creating and sharing instructional materials. Often ID specialists also seek input into instructional solutions and provide constructive feedback to team members on projects during development. Thus, they also require refined skill sets in presenting instructional ideas, orally communicating with project stakeholders, collaboration and consensus-building, negotiation and conflict resolution, questioning, and active listening.

It is the responsibility of the ID specialist to assure the integrity of an instructional solution's design. Thus, a primary role of the ID specialist is to apply systems thinking to instructional design and performance improvement projects. This includes referencing best practices in ID research, theory, and practices and applying ID and other disciplines' principles to the design of instructional products. To do these tasks well, the ID specialist also maintains a broad social network with other professionals and continually develops his or her own knowledge and skills in technologies relevant to instructional interventions.

The ID specialist is also well versed in data collection and analysis competencies in order to design instructional solutions based on identified needs and evaluate instruction throughout development and implementation phases. Generally the ID specialist will work with an analyst or evaluator who conducts these types of tasks; the ID specialist then uses results to design and enhance product specifications.

Finally, the ID specialist has a keen sense of, and respect for, the intellectual property rights of others and regulatory guidelines and organization policies. They take the responsibility to make sure that all materials and references adhere to ethical, legal, and political guidelines in the workplace.

Planning and Analysis

The most critical competencies in this domain for ID specialists include: conducting the needs assessment and selecting and using analysis techniques for determining instructional content. The competencies that are secondary to the ID specialist in this domain include: identifying and describing target population and environmental characteristics (including technology) and analyzing these characteristics to design instruction.

The ID specialist is responsible for the needs assessment process that eventually leads to the definition of design solutions. It is critical that the ID specialist be able to define the nature of the learning or performance problems; this ultimately defines the nature of the instruction. The ID specialist also must use the needs assessment data to identify the root causes of performance issues; suggesting that a performance issue occurs because of a gap in knowledge, skills, or attitudes (those things that can be corrected with instruction) or not. From this determination the ID specialist then synthesizes all of the information and recommends instruction and noninstructional solutions. Thus, it is through communication and data collection competencies and refined knowledge of design and learning that the ID specialist can identify performance issues (and their causes) and propose appropriate solutions.

Working with an analyst, the ID specialist plays a role in describing the target population, characteristics of the environment, infrastructure to support design and implementation, and organizational factors that may impact proposed instructional solutions. The primary activity of the ID specialist is to synthesize all of the gather information to design the proposed instructional solution. The ID specialist (with a subject matter expert) also takes a primary role in determining the scope, validity, and flow of content presentation in the proposed instruction. This includes analyzing existing instruction to determine adequacy of content, instruction, and learning and determining subordinate and prerequisite skills and knowledge required by the target audience.

Finally, selecting appropriate technologies capable of enhancing the impact of the instruction is a critical role of the ID specialist in collaboration with an instructional technologies or e-learning specialist. Together they identify technologies, define their use in delivering or supporting instruction and learning, and assess the benefits and limitations of the technologies given the proposed instruction, learning environment, and organizational characteristics. Thus, ID specialists must have a grasp of available technologies, their features and characteristics, benefits and challenges of their implementation, and infrastructure requirements.

Design and Development

The most critical competencies in this domain for ID specialists include: organizing instructional programs and/or products, designing instructional interventions, selecting or modifying existing instructional materials, developing instructional materials, and designing learning assessment. The competencies that are secondary to the ID specialist in this domain include: using appropriate design and development processes and planning noninstructional interventions.

Although the ID manager is primarily responsible for identifying and managing the design and development processes, the ID specialist often takes the responsibility (under the supervision of the ID Manager) to modify the ID process as project parameters change over time. ID specialists should be well able to rationalize major changes or minor modifications based on their knowledge of the ID process and current their project.

The greatest impact the ID specialist provides on an instructional project is in the design and development of instructional interventions. ID specialist have highly developed competencies in organizing instructional project and products based on project scope. They are able to successfully define and sequence instructional goals and specify and sequence anticipated learning outcomes. They often work with a subject matter expert to organize content and define required performance outcomes. The ID specialist is also an expert at identifying instructional strategies that prompt learners to interaction with content in ways that support learning outcomes. ID specialists have strong knowledge of how to design activities and resources that incorporate message and visual design, motivational and interactive learning principles, and accommodate social, cultural, political, and other factors that may influence learning. They are also, as suggested above, knowledgeable about a variety of technology and media and able to select those that are best able to enhance the proposed instructional intervention. Technology choices are often made in conjunction with an instructional technologies and information about the organization's technology infrastructure.

Although the primary focus of the ID specialist is in designing instructional interventions, often needs assessment will suggest that performance issues are not a matter of knowledge, skill, or attitude gaps.

Rather, the problems are caused by lack of information, incentive or disincentive issues, lack of or poor quality tools, or a variety of other issues. Given the knowledge gained during the needs assessment process and understanding of the relationships among instruction and performance, the ID specialist is often involved also in designing noninstructional solutions. Thus, the ID specialist may advise clients on noninstructional solutions such as changes in job descriptions, design of information systems and management information systems or HR policies, as their expertise and comfort allows.

Often, a needs assessment will identify instruction already existing in an organization that is deemed *not fully effective* or identify holes in current instruction that need to be filled. In some situations the existing instruction can be enhanced. In some situations packaged instruction can be purchase *as-is* or with *customization options*. ID specialist can help to identify when existing materials should be modified or replaced. Once chosen, the ID specialist can help to validate the choice and integrate the enhanced or new instructional resources into the proposed overall design.

ID specialists also play a role in developing instructional materials. Although often the novice instructional designers and technology specialists play a major role in actually constructing instructional interventions based on design specifications, the ID specialist generally creates the specification and oversee novices and technicians making sure that all materials follow specification and alight with analysis. This activity suggests that ID specialists have strong collaboration competencies as they work with both novice designers and production specialists.

Finally, in collaboration with evaluators, the ID specialist exhibits strong learning assessment competencies. The ID specialist takes a primary role in identify the learning processes and outcomes to be measured and performs constant reviews of all materials to assure that assessments align with instructional goals, learning outcomes, and instructional strategies.

Evaluation and Implementation

The most critical competencies in this domain for ID specialists include: revising instructional solutions based on data and implement, disseminate, and diffuse interventions. The competency that is secondary to the ID specialist in this domain is evaluate interventions.

The ID specialist consults and collaborates heavily with evaluators and instructional technologists during this part of the instructional design and development process. The ID specialist will provide input on the evaluation plans and take a secondary role during summative evaluation, however takes a primary role in the implementation of formative evaluation.

It is during the formative evaluation processes that the ID specialist actively interprets results from formative evaluation to make decisions about final enhancements to the intervention.

When instruction is transitioned into full implementation the ID specialist's role is diminished to tasks that support creation of a change vision that aligns learning and performance goals with organizations goals and identifying subsequent modifications to implementation, dissemination, and diffusion processes. At this point the ID specialist will generally collaborate with an program evaluator at points where revisions are suggested based on summative evaluation.

Management

ID specialists, when an ID manager is present, play secondary roles in managing instructional projects. ID specialists will support efforts to maintain effective relationships between the design team and the stakeholders and conduct project reviews. The ID specialist also supports the ID manager establish project scope and write proposals for instructional design projects. In the case of projects with no formal ID manager, the ID specialist uses management competencies to scope, facilitate, manage, and administer projects.

THE INSTRUCTIONAL DESIGN MANAGER

ID managers are generally responsible for controlling, administering, and directing an organization's ID function. As indicated in Table 5.1, in the 2012 ID competencies there are 36 primary performance statements and 9 secondary performance statement across 11 competencies clustered in 4 general domains that define the ID manager. Together, these competencies reflect the complexity of instructional design managers role. It is important to note that competent ID managers also have a grasp of the instructional design process and all its intricacies.

Overall, ID managers are held accountable by the organization's leaders for the accomplishments of the ID function ensuring that it aligns with, and supports, other parts of the organization in meeting the organization's goals. ID managers set the tone and work agenda for ID employees and consultants. ID managers hopefully began their careers as an ID specialist where they gained knowledge and the expertise to lead the organization's ID efforts. However, often those who serve as the ID function manager are human resources generalists who may not have a complete grasp of ID, learning, and performance improvement. Thus, this set of ID competencies may be very helpful preparing ID managers for this role.

Given ID managers multiple relationships and responsibilities, it is not surprising that they should have competencies in the following domains

- *Professional foundations*, with a primary emphasis on communications skills and applying research and theory to the discipline of instructional design and a secondary emphasis responding to ethical, legal, and political implications in the workplace.
- *Design and development*, with primary emphasis using appropriate design and development processes, organizing instructional programs, planning noninstructional interventions, making decisions to modify existing instructional products.
- *Evaluation and implementation*, with primary emphasis implementing and evaluating instruction.
- *Management*, with a primary emphasis on applying management skills in the ID function, managing partnerships and collaborative relationships, and planning and managing instructional design projects.

Professional Foundations

As with all those involved in the ID function, the ID manager should be able to communicate effectively in visual, oral, and written form. The ID manager must also be able to apply systems thinking in organizing and defining project scope. Most importantly the ID manager is usually the gatekeeper in matters of ethical, legal, and political implications of design in the workplace

ID managers are responsible for making connections to other stakeholders in the organization. They work closely with the managers of such operational functions such as manufacturing, supply chain, and sales and with the managers of such support functions such as finance, legal, and information technology. In these capacities knowledge of the design function and systems thinking are particularly important. ID managers also work with and represent the ID experts who report to them. The ID managers strong communication skills are important because these stakeholders often will attempt to address organizational issues using performance frameworks, points of view, and language that are unique to other parts of the organization.

ID managers also engage other organization stakeholders in understanding the ID issues and negotiating solutions. Such engagement involves two-way dialogue that occurs one-on-one or in groups in either face-to-face meetings or through virtual communication vehicles. The dialogue can be visual, written, and verbal or a combination of the three forms of communication. Such exchange consists of sharing opinions, listening to and understating other points of view, and inviting feedback. It also can include delivering presentations and reports that effectively share the intended messages.

It is also expected that ID managers can foresee and direct ID processes and outcomes. Because such insight and skilled maneuvering requires more than individual expertise, ID managers have up-to-date knowledge of the research and theory related to the discipline of ID and can explain to the other stakeholders the key concepts and principles related to instructional design. ID managers use systems thinking to gain insight into both the intended and unintended consequences of actions.

Finally, the ID manager is should have competencies to identify and respond to ethical, legal, and political implications of design in the workplace. These skills are a secondary emphasis of ID manager in most situations. However, in today's dynamic work environment, various situations arise that have ethical implications. It is therefore prudent for the ID manager to develop strong competencies the ethical, legal, and political guidelines of the organization and use these when making ID function and project decisions.

Design and Development

It is the responsibility of the ID manager to direct ID efforts, which includes determining the ID processes used within the ID function and organize the instructional programs and products that will be developed. ID managers will work with ID specialists and/or instructional technologists to assure that processes for each effort are appropriate based on the nature of the project and that the instructional design process is modified as needed to reflect changes in the project parameters. The ID manager will also work with ID specialists and/or instructional technologists to determine the overall scope of selected projects.

Often a needs assessment will suggest that a noninstructional intervention (e.g., incentive modification, equipment requirements, process issues, organizational modifications) is necessary. Most often the ID managers will negotiate with key stakeholders (e.g., manager who owns the need, the organization's executives, and external consultants) to identify these interventions and determine the kind of effort that will best address the organizational needs (e.g., performance support, knowledge management, personnel selection, job redesign, incentive systems). The

ID manager will often consult with ID specialists and instructional technology, e-learning specialists, as appropriate, who may help justify the need for a noninstructional solution and engage in developing design specification for the intervention. Note that instruction may play a support role in such noninstructional interventions. For example, a knowledge management program could be rolled out via training.

Evaluation and Implementation

In this domain, the primary competency for ID managers is implement, disseminate, and diffuse instructional and noninstructional interventions. Given the ID manager's role in directing an organization's ID function, it is not surprising that ID managers are skilled in creating a vision of change that aligns learning and performance goals with organizational goals; planning for the implementation and disseminations of interventions; or that they monitor the implementation, dissemination, and diffusion progress. ID managers will collaborate with the ID specialists and instructional technologist/e-learning specialist in creating a vision.

Management

By definition, the ID manager's primary competencies include those within the management domain including: applying business skills to managing the instructional design function, managing partnerships and collaborative relationships, and planning and managing instructional design projects.

The ID manager should be competence in basic business skills. This involves assuring that the ID function supports the larger organization, has high quality processes and products, uses resources appropriately, has the personnel and expertise to accomplish the function's goals, and is understood and valued by management and other stakeholders. The ID manager should also be able to market instructional design services within the organization and manage ID customer relations.

ID managers should also be able to successfully manage partnerships and collaborative relationships reflecting the importance of achieving performance goals by working with other stakeholders. ID managers often are responsible for identifying stakeholders and their level of contribution to a process/project. They also will build connections among ID professionals and other stakeholders, and effectively manage cross functional teams. In addition, ID managers must be competence in conducting project reviews throughout and at the end of a project and conduct stakeholder reviews, ultimately determining success and areas for improvement in projects and personnel.

It is critical that ID managers be able to successfully plan and manage instructional design projects within the ID function. In ID projects, ID managers often work with the ID specialist and instructional technologists to establish project scope and goals and write proposal for ID projects. The ID manager will be able to use a variety of planning and managing tools (e.g., project management tools, cost/benefit tools, recourse allocation tools timelines, etc.) to support overall management of ID function projects and make appropriate choices for allocating project resources to support plans. It is also expected that ID managers have the competencies to managing multiple priorities and, as necessary, identify and address project issues.

THE ANALYST/EVALUATOR

The analyst/evaluator can play multiple roles in an instructional design project. As analysts, they specialize in the conduct, analysis, and interpretation of performance analyses and needs assessments. Such activities typically occur at the "front end" of the instructional design process. As evaluators, they work in all project phases—planning for the evaluation early in the project, conducting formative evaluations during design and development, and conducting summative evaluations during and following the implementation. As indicated in Table 5.1, in the 2012 ID competencies there are 29 primary performance statements and 10 secondary performance across 14 competencies clustered in 5 general domains that define the analyst/evaluator. Together, these competencies reflect the complexity of the instructional analyst's/evaluator's role. The analyst/evaluator competencies relate to:

- *Professional foundations*, with primary emphasis on communication and research skills
- *Planning and analysis*, with primary emphasis on identifying learner and environmental characteristics and conducting and reporting needs assessment
- *Design and development*, with primary attention to designing learning assessments
- *Implementation and evaluation*, with primary emphasis on planning and implementing formative and summative evaluations
- *Management*, with a supporting emphasis in conducting project reviews and in writing proposals for design projects

Professional Foundation Skills

The analyst/evaluator, like all instructional designers, are dependent upon a broad range of foundational skills. Because of the specialized role in gathering information from people and in distilling and presenting that information to others as part of the evaluation effort, an important area of competence for the analyst/evaluator involves communication skills.

A high level of competence in communication skills is critical to the analyst/evaluator for two major reasons. First, data collected through interviews, focus groups, and surveys become the foundation for all major design, development, and revision decisions; such data collection involves effective questioning techniques and, for the interviews and focus groups, active listening skills. Second, the analyst/evaluator must be able to clearly articulate in written form any interpretations and recommendations based on the findings.

Almost all of the communication performance statements are considered primary for the analyst/evaluator. These center on the need to interact with individuals and diverse groups throughout the organization when gathering data and insights into "what is really happening." Active listening is an especially important competency. The analyst/evaluator interacts with individuals and groups when gathering information. The ability to listen and actually "hear" what informants are saying is critical.

In the needs assessment of an ID project, the analyst/evaluator must lay aside any preconceived ideas about the issues at hand. Instead, the person must rely on active listening and expert facilitation skills to uncover data about optimal and actual performance and root causes of the problem. Discussions may reveal issues pertaining to motivation and openness to change, work environment factors that may affect the choice of the intervention, and the target group's attitudes to potential solutions, including delivery systems.

At the conclusion of the data collection for a needs assessment or evaluation effort, the analyst/evaluator must prepare a report and in many cases also make a formal presentation of the findings to stakeholder groups. The person must prepare crisp, well-written, well-documented reports using tabular and graphical displays of data. Reports should be written in the client's language rather than that of instructional design, in order to gain the attention and understanding of management decision makers as well as other stakeholder groups.

The analyst/evaluator requires a high level of expertise in making a well-reasoned and compelling case for change. Presentations to senior management and other stakeholders must be informative, engaging, and persuasive, convincing them that the proposed solutions are compatible with, and responsive to, the needs and goals of the organization. Recommendations should be data-based, but the analyst/evaluator also needs the "people" skills to gain support for these recommendations.

The instructional designer or design team represents one of the analyst's/evaluator's primary customers. Team members use the findings and recommendations to make significant design and development decisions. The team requires clearly communicated information about the learner group characteristics and environmental and cultural factors that may need to be accommodated in the design and development process, as well as the anticipated degree of support for the specific interventions. Furthermore, when undertaking revisions, the design team relies on evaluation data, interpretation, and recommendations.

Likewise, the design team is likely to depend on the analyst/evaluator for debriefing them to establish project lessons learned. Since evaluations are usually undertaken some time after the instructional event, face-to-face meetings between the design team and the analyst/evaluator are generally necessary to discuss the report and gain insights from the evaluation. Such meetings can be used to enhance future instructional development as well as suggest revisions in a program.

The core of the analyst/evaluator's work involves data collection and analysis. Whether as part of a needs assessment or part of an evaluation, this person seeks to uncover any issues or problems. The analyst/evaluator role requires a high level of skills in identifying the needed data, designing data collection tools and procedures, collecting the data, and using the appropriate quantitative and qualitative methods to analyze the data. Only with such skills can the data collection and analysis uncover the relevant issues and generate data that are comprehensive and representative of the target group.

The analyst/evaluator needs to be skilled in formulating questions and conducting interviews and focus groups. It is also important for this specialist to be aware of cultural attitudes that may influence the responses. In some cultures, it is unacceptable to express opinions that differ from the most senior person in the group. In this situation, a written or online survey is more likely to provide more reliable and valid data than a focus group. In other cultures, respondents tend to choose the midpoint on a Likert-type scale survey regardless of their real views.

The analyst/evaluator must be able to use basic statistical techniques to analyze the data that have been collected. When using surveys to gather data globally, thought should be given as to whether translations are needed for any countries or groups of respondents. If so, there should be a translation into that other language by one person and a back-translation into the initial language by another, independent person. If an English language survey is used worldwide, every effort should be made to communicate in unambiguous English, avoiding Western terms or jargon and using simple sentence structures. When employing online surveys using an organizations system, the analyst/evaluator may need to partner with information technology specialists or external vendors for needed technical support.

Planning and Analysis

The analyst/evaluator plays a major role in planning and analysis for an instructional design project. Much of this is considered "up-front" work, and it lays the foundation for the remainder of the project. The specialist's role focuses on conducting the needs assessment, describing learner and environmental characteristics, and conducting analyses to determine instructional content and use of instructional technologies.

Needs assessment and analysis are foundational to the entire instructional design process and they represent critical facets of the analyst/evaluator's role. As part of the needs assessment process, the analyst/evaluator must accurately describe the dimensions of current performance, identify the root causes of performance or attitudinal discrepancies, and recommend interventions to close the performance gap. The analyst also prepares a cost-benefit analysis for recommended solutions when required by a stakeholder or client.

The analyst/evaluator writes a performance analysis report after carefully reviewing all data and then proposes and advocates a range of solutions including both instructional and noninstructional ones, as appropriate. Even a variety of training interventions may be proposed for some performance gaps. Performance analysis and needs assessment of this caliber goes beyond confirming senior management's dictates or learners' requests, because they are based on an in-depth assessment of the relationship between current performance and desired organizational outputs.

A clear description of the target population, including the current skill level, is a key output of the analyst/evaluator's work. In performance analysis and needs assessment, the analyst/evaluator must identify who needs the intervention and report on learner characteristics that the design team should consider. These considerations typically include such demographics as cultural diversity, language fluency, learning preferences, variations in entry-level knowledge across regions, level of motivation to change, and capability with relevant technologies.

The analyst/evaluator must recognize environmental factors that can influence the success of the intervention. That person identifies systemic issues that should be taken into account during the design and development phases. These same environmental factors may influence the attitudes of the learners toward the training and may positively or negatively impact the transfer of learning to the workplace. In highlighting work processes, structures or systemic factors that may undermine effective implementation of training, the analyst/evaluator is also looking ahead to the environmental factors that undermine the postimplementation effects of the intervention. Examples include a lack of facilities or resources to deliver the training, lack of supervisor support for the intervention, an organizational culture that undermines the training, the need for job redesign prior to training, a lack of supporting processes, the selection of underqualified new hires or lack of support by the trainees' managers. The analyst/evaluator is concerned with the transfer of training to the work environment and the long-term impact of an intervention on the organization. These conclusions are dependent upon data from a variety of sources. The analyst/evaluator documents any identified barriers as well as notes drivers or environmental factors that support the intervention and overall impact on stakeholders performance.

The analyst/evaluator is the specialist who assists the design team in gathering and analyzing content from subject-matter experts and from other sources. The focus of such efforts is to help determine the instructional content and the appropriate use of any instructional technologies. This analysis takes into account the current levels of content knowledge to determine what may be needed in training. The analysis also takes into account the current and available technologies as well as emerging technologies and assesses the benefits and limitations of each. The results of this analysis may be provided to the instructional technologist on the team for further refinement.

Design and Development

The primary role for the analyst/evaluator during design and development focus on the cons-benefit analysis related to existing instructional materials and the design and development of learning assessments. When an ID project identifies that there are existing instructional materials that are not effective or appropriate one decision is whether they should be modified or replaced with other instruction, either developed or purchased. The analyst/evaluator can conduct a cost/benefit analysis to support this decision.

The most critical role that the analyst/evaluator plays in the design and development phase however is consulting on the development of learning assessments. First the specialist works with the ID and instructional technologist specialists to identify and define the learning processes and outcomes to be measured. Based on that identification, the specialist can construct methods to measure those processes and outcomes. Unlike other design team members, the analyst/evaluator also possesses the skills to undertake the appropriate analyses to determine the reliability and validity of those assessments. Ultimately, these assessment must be aligned with the instructional and strategies.

Implementation and Evaluation

Evaluation skills form the second major cluster of competence for the analyst/evaluator. Many think of evaluation as taking place at the end of the intervention, but the competent analyst/evaluator understands and communicates the importance of beginning in the early stages of the design process. The specialist plans both the assessment and evaluation strategies in partnership with others on the design team.

Formative, developmental, and summative evaluation strategies (including impact and cost-benefit analyses) are developed at a macrolevel, taking into account the environmental and culture issues previously discussed. With formative and development evaluations, the specialist must provide timely information to the design team so that appropriate revisions can be implemented. At the conclusion of the training implementation, the analyst/evaluator meets with stakeholders to present the findings and discuss recommendations. The stakeholder group may include management, the design team, instructors, content specialists, and developers. Organizational development specialists may also take on the stakeholder role, if the evaluation identifies organizational resistance to change.

The analyst/evaluator is concerned with the transfer of training to the work environment and the long-term impact of an intervention on the organization. These conclusions are dependent upon data from a variety of sources. They also build upon the initial needs assessment, especially when that assessment identified factors that the organization expected to be impacted by the intervention. When the intervention is implemented globally, evaluation decisions must be reflective of the diverse environmental and the social, cultural, and physical influences that can impact both the delivery and the outcomes of training. The analyst/evaluator must be sensitive to the impact of cultural differences on learning, performance, and long-term transfer. In many cases, the impact of these systemic factors cannot be anticipated or predicted, because organizations lack a history of comprehensive program evaluation on a global basis. Similarly, the effects of organizational culture must be taken into account. Organizational values and culture can support or undermine the intervention, leading to success or failure. The competent analyst/evaluator is mindful of these issues and attempts to assess their influence.

The analyst's/evaluator's recommendations must always relate to the organization's strategic goals and the changes needed to achieve these goals. For this specialist, focusing on the strategic goals is particularly important when findings do not support the prevailing view of a particular intervention. For example, evaluation data may show that a popular program is having no impact on work practices or that the cost of the intervention outweighs the benefits. In such cases, the findings may be discounted, challenged, or even refuted by the instructional developers, the subject-matter experts, the instructors, the primary customers, or management. It is up to the analyst/evaluator to present persuasive arguments that will counteract such opinions.

Management

The competency of primary importance within this domain for the analyst/evaluator is that of working with stakeholders. The specialist depends on the support and input of internal people, and occasionally external experts or contractors, to obtain the performance analysis data and insights needed to identify critical performance issues, root causes, and a range of potential solutions. In some organizations, performance analysis and needs assessment may be regarded as time wasters and unnecessary. The skilled analyst/evaluator is able to identify the key stakeholders and persuade them, especially senior management, that analysis is imperative and a sound investment of time and money. The analyst/evaluator must also build collaborative relationships with potential subject matter experts during the data collection phases. Content experts often agree to act as project SMEs on the basis of relationships formed during the needs assessment phase.

THE E-LEARNING SPECIALIST/INSTRUCTIONAL TECHNOLOGIST (IT)

The e-learning/IT specialist's profile is almost identical to that of the ID specialist, however includes demonstrated expertise on technology-based and supported instructional products. As indicated in Table 5.1, in the 2012 ID competencies there are 40 primary performance statements (6 more than the ID specialist) and 33 secondary performance (6 less than the ID specialist) across 21 competencies clustered in 5 general domains that define the e-learning specialist. Together, these competencies reflect the complexity of the e-learning specialist's role.

The e-learning specialist six primary performances that are different from the ID specialist all focus on the expectation for advance technology knowledge and skills. e-learning specialists work in all phases of an instructional project. However, a majority of their work is dedicated to the development of technology aspects of instructional interventions. For larger projects there may be several specialists working together to fulfill this role. The e-learning specialist competencies are found in the following domains:

- *Professional foundations*, with a particular emphasis on communications skills, applying concepts, techniques, and theories of other disciplines to technology-based learning and performance improvements, systems thinking, updating current knowledge of new technologies, and intellectual property rights
- *Planning and analysis*, with particular emphasis on identifying performance problems, learner, environmental and infrastructure characteristics and best practices in using technologies
- *Design and development*, with particular emphasis on selecting appropriate technologies and designing and producing instructional interventions to support interaction, learning, and assessment with the most effective technologies
- *Evaluation and implementation*, with particular emphasis on formative evaluation and revision of technology-based or supported interventions
- *Management*, with a particular emphasis maintaining project scope, focus, and schedules and on collaborative relationships with other team members in the design and development of technology solutions

Professional Foundations

A majority of the communication competencies are primary skills of the e-learning specialist, similar to those of the ID specialist. It is particularly important that e-learning specialists also maintain strong competencies in applying concepts, techniques, and theory of other disciplines (e.g., message design, visual design) to learning and performance improvements interventions that use technologies. As with the ID specialist, the e-learning specialist should also use systems thinking to help define technology-based or supported instructional solutions.

With the continued growth in new technologies and digital tools is it expected that e-learning specialists will constantly update their knowledge of emerging technologies or technology uses in instructional and learning settings and have more advanced skills in using such technologies in practice over the ID specialists. Nowadays, or even in the early days when computer technologies began to emerge in educational settings, a trend is for digital tools (e.g., computers, interactive video, internet, electronic white boards, mobile technologies, response systems) to be put in place with little thought about the instructional implications, those that are beneficial and those that can be inhibiting. Little attention is traditionally paid to the features of new technologies to support or inhibit teaching and learning. Therefore, it is essential that e-learning specialists play gatekeeper and persuader in responding to haphazard integration of technology resources. Advising on the long-term strengths and weaknesses as well as cost/benefits of using technologies based on learning needs is important in developing instructional interventions that have any ability to improve performance.

Given the ease of accessing and capturing information and resources from others in this technologically sophisticated world suggests that another essential competency for the e-learning specialist is recognizing and respecting intellectual property rights of others. The e-learning specialist should know and maintain ethical and legal perspective when it comes to uses of digital resources created by others. Even in cases of international projects where copyright laws do not exist, it is important that the E-learning specialist observe ethical practices.

Planning and Analysis

The e-learning specialists competencies are identical to the ID specialist in the Planning and Analysis domain with the exception of three performance statements. The e-learning specialist has primary (as opposed to the ID specialists secondary) emphasis on identifying the infrastructure that is available to support design and deliver of instruction, describing the capabilities of existing and emerging technologies required to enhance the impact of instruction, and assess the benefits and limitations of existing and emerging technologies. e-learning specialists will generally have additional training, therefore knowledge and skills, in instructional technology that will provide additional benefits to instructional design project teams. Such competencies will help in the identification of appropriate technology solutions based on the needs assessment. e-learning specialists knowledge of multiple types of technologies will also be useful in identify which technologies make the best sense (and should be proposed) and which features of these best choices are most likely to fulfill instructional and learning needs.

Design and Development

The e-learning specialists competencies are identical to the ID specialist in this domain with the exception of one performance statement, selecting appropriate technology and media to enhance instructional interventions, taking into account theory, research, and practical factors.

e-learning specialists require expertise and competencies in all facets of the design and development of technology-based learning including use of color, interactivity, screen design, motivational characteristics, graphics, overall message design, and social connectedness factors. Although message and visual design are both critical in all instruction, the varying features and views of instruction in different types of technologies (e.g., computer monitors, smaller handheld devices) suggest changes in information structures, presentation, level of interactivity, and other characteristics. Thus, the competencies of the e-learning specialist can ensure that design specifications effectively integrate these new technologies based on overall instructional goals, expected learning outcomes, accessible resources, and technology infrastructure.

e-learning specialists, as ID specialists, must also be proficient in building connections among technology and nontechnology aspects of an instructional product. This is especially important in the cases of blended learning environments and in the transfer of learning from instruction to the realities of practice. Nowadays, rarely is face-to-face instruction not accompanied by some type of online information, instruction, or learning. e-learning specialists should be able to provide valuable input on aspects of instruction that are best delivered or available in digital format or that require asynchronous activities or that require synchronous interactions with those in distance locations. Developing an effective design should take into account how the learners (and facilitator) will interact with all resources for the instruction whether paper, technology, and human. e-learning specialists should have an understanding of all aspects of instruction and implementation of instruction with regards to technology-based and supported learning.

e-learning specialists should also be able to provide input on technology choices that will support post-instruction transfer of new knowledge to the workplace. Often training has some level of disconnect between training and work environments. Technology solutions may help to bring learning and practice together by using tools that are the 'same' during instruction as those used during work or using instructional resources that are easily and safely accessed in the workplace as references after instruction. e-learning specialists should develop a keen sense of the types of technology resources that are used in the practices of the target audience for instruction and use their knowledge of technology to help the ID specialists create instructional solutions that support transfer (with these tools) from instructional to practice environments.

In the case of the emerging mobile and handheld technologies, for example, e-learning specialists must be skilled at reducing technical content to clear and unambiguous text for various deliver mechanisms. They must be able to design multimedia interfaces that are effective and visually stimulate the interest of the learner without compromising the instructional and learning requirements. Technology-based instruction may entertain users, but its principle function is to contribute to learning and improve performance often in multi-cultural settings. Thus the e-learning specialist partners with the ID specialist to design and develop technology solutions that are most likely to support learning and transfer.

Evaluation and Implementation

The e-learning specialists competencies are identical to the ID specialist in evaluation and implementation. Both should be well versed in basic evaluation techniques, abilities to revise interventions based on evaluative data, and knowledgeable of the best techniques and strategies to implement instructional interventions. The e-learning specialist will be focused on the technology based aspects of the instructional interventions during these phases, working also with the analyst/evaluator to identify and gather data on specific technology resources.

Management

The e-learning specialists competencies are identical to the ID specialist in the management domain. Both play a supportive role in managing partnerships and collaborative relationships and planning and managing instructional design projects. The e-learning specialist will be focused on providing technology perspectives during collaborations and projects reviews. The e-learning specialist will also provide relevant input on project scope and goals based on their advanced knowledge of the design and development of technology based and support instructional interventions. Thoughts on development process, resources, and time lines may be particularly important in determining overall project scope and progress.

Development of technology resources, given the effort required to develop such resources, may also require additional steps in the design, development, and implementation steps not normally required with classroom or paper-based instruction, for example, technology testing and error reviews). It is critical that the e-learning specialist brings these tasks into the management plan early in the planning stages to avoid time line and resource issues later in the project.

SUMMARY

The instructional design profession has expanded over the decades to include a variety of specialties. All of these specialists (ID, manager, analyst/evaluator, e-learning) and others, have painted the role of the instructional designer based on specified interests and primary competencies. However, it is suggested that all instructional designers, specialists and generalists, should maintain basic competencies in all of the instructional designer domains. Although the descriptions in this chapter lean toward circumstances of large projects with multiple ID specialists working together in a team, many times an instructional designer works solo, fully creating an instructional solution or working on different aspects of an instructional project, taking responsibility for all of these roles. This is often the case of an instructional design consultant or contractor who is hired for a specific instructional project, oftentimes with limited scope.

Whether working in a team or solo, instructional designers have a great deal to learn to be competent. Specialists like program evaluators or e-learning specialists, also must be competent in the all aspects of design and development, however have keenly developed competencies in their area of interest. Competent instructional designers, whether generalists or specialists, develop through education, experience, and participation in on-going professional development. Table 5.1 gives an overview of the competencies that an instructional design specialist, instructional design manager, analyst/evaluator, and e-learning specialists should have to take on their respective roles. The Table 5.1 may also be helpful in identifying the primary and secondary competencies for those who are hiring or contracting generalists and specialists—and those instructional designers who are contemplating assignments or new positions.

CHAPTER 6

THE COMPETENCY
VALIDATION RESEARCH

This chapter describes the research involved in the development and validation of the ibstpi instructional designer competencies. These competencies, as with the other ibstpi competency sets, reflect a current
assessment of what active professionals do in their practice. Such an
assessment, far from being the opinion of a few individuals who claim to
be experts or a trendy online survey in social media circles, is the product
of rigorous research methods and a legacy of research studies, as
described below. Over time these studies have increased the number of
active professionals consulted, across continents, countries, languages,
diverse organizations settings, levels of expertise, and degrees of formal
education in the discipline. Indeed, ibstpi has set a benchmark for this
type of research as there are no other studies with this level of rigor and
scope.

The ibstpi ID competencies are empirically-based. They are grounded
in several research studies, including:

- The development of the 1986 ibstpi ID competencies of "journeyman" instructional designers;
- The Atchison (1996) study that identified competencies of expert
  instructional designers;
- The Song (1998) study that sought to replicate the work of Atchison;

- The development of the 2000 ibstpi ID competencies that distinguished "essential" from "advanced" performance tasks;
- The validation research for the 2012 ibstpi ID competencies.

This chapter includes an overview of the formal research that was instrumental in the construction of the present set of competencies, including the previous studies and the present ibstpi validation study and its findings.

THE FOUNDATIONAL RESEARCH

The 1986 ibstpi ID Competencies

The ibstpi board grew from the work of the Joint Certification Task Force, which was composed of the Association for Education Communications and Technology (AECT) and the National Society for Performance and Instruction (NSPI, now the International Society for Performance Improvement, ISPI). The Task Force developed the initial set of competencies for the instructional design profession, published an index linking current publications to competencies, and created a prototype assessment procedure. The Task Force reorganized itself in 1983 to avoid conflicts of interest with its parent organizations.

Work on the 1986 ID competencies was focused on describing a "journeyman" instructional designer. Such a person may or may not have had formal academic training in the field but probably did have considerable training, experience, and exposure to the literature in the field. The level of proficiency was taken to represent someone with at least 3 years of experience.

THE ATCHISON STUDY

The following section begins by describing the purpose and procedures for this study. We then describe the results and the application of those results to the work by the ibstpi team.

Purpose and Procedures

Rowland (1992) argued that there had been little systematic study as to what design practitioners actually did and that this impeded the field's ability to provide an accurate description of instructional design practice. Further, he suggested that this description of design practice should be approached by looking at designers with a range of expertise. Atchison's (1996) study, as a response to Rowland, sought to identify the professional competencies of expert instructional designers by examining the knowledge, skills, and attitudes used to analyze instructional design problems, to implement design solutions, and to evaluate design effectiveness.

Atchison's (1996) study used a critical incident method. His data were gathered from extensive interviews of 15 expert designers in four different work settings—higher education and vocational trade, business and industry, health care, and government. The resulting data were analyzed to identify common themes.

Results

All the designers agreed that they needed to know the core design skills and processes of instructional systems design. In addition, though, they were engaged in other related activities. Nine competency "themes" emerged from the analysis:

1. Demonstrates attributes of reflective practice.
2. Recognizes ethical issues in instructional design practice and is able to formulate an effective response.
3. Demonstrates humanistic qualities.
4. Demonstrates collaborative skills in instructional systems design.
5. Effectively advocates the legitimacy of instructional design practice to the client population.
6. Articulates and demonstrates an active commitment to maintaining the stability of evaluation systems in instructional design.
7. Understands components of and effectively interacts with a business environment.
8. Understands and effectively uses marketing principles to promote instructional design services.
9. Is able to effectively diffuse innovative instructional design programs into various settings.

Application of These Findings

The 2000 ibstpi competency development team used Atchison's (1996) study as a basis for the development of the initial competency set that was validated. The 2000 ibstpi competencies, in turn, were reviewed and revised for the present set of instructional design competencies.

THE SONG STUDY

The following section begins by describing the purpose and procedures for this study. We then describe the results and the application of those results to the work by the ibstpi team.

Purpose and Procedures

The Song (1998) study examined ID competencies in the training and instructional design profession. Specifically, it investigated the perceptions of practicing professionals as to the 1986 ibstpi ID competencies. Song also used Atchison's (1996) nine competency themes as a foundation for developing expert competencies to complete her survey instrument. The focus was to determine if this expanded list of competencies was valid, and if a respondent group of practitioners could determine the level of expertise of ID competencies.

The study used a survey method, with the 1986 ibstpi competencies and the expert themes forming the basis for the survey. The study gathered the participant's perceptions of the level of complexity (novice, intermediate, and expert level) and the validity of the competencies. Eighty surveys were mailed to members of the Minnesota chapter of ISPI and the St. Cloud Minnesota Chapter of ASTD.

Results

Of the 80 surveys, 33 were completed and eight were partially completed, for a 51% response rate. Nearly three fourths of the respondents worked in business, government, and higher education settings with Master's degrees and experience in ID or related fields. The Song (1998) study reestablished that the competencies derived from Atchison's expert themes were valid, and the practitioners rated these competencies at the expert level, with the exception of two which were rated at the intermediate level.

Application of These Findings

The Song study provided the ibstpi board with valuable data to assist in future revisions of the ID competencies. In particular, it indicated the need for some sort of expertise levels that would be needed in future sets of ID competencies. It also provided evidence that some competency areas, such as communication and needs assessment, were perceived as essential for all instructional designers.

THE 2000 IBSTPI ID COMPETENCIES

This section describes the purpose and procedures for the 2000 ibstpi study. Then the results and the application of those results to the current work are presented.

Purpose and Procedures

The purpose of the 2000 ibstpi study was to examine a revision of the 1986 competencies and to determine the levels of expertise required on the job for each of the competencies and performance statements. Two separate surveys were developed: one measured designer perceptions of competency criticality, and the second determined the levels of expertise typically required on the job. The criticality survey used a 5-point Likert-type scale, with 5 indicating very high criticality and 1 indicating not critical at all. There were 83 respondents to the expertise survey and 93 to the criticality survey, with most respondents from the United States and Canada.

Results

In general, the respondents gave high criticality ratings to the competencies and performance statements. Only one of the 23 competencies received a rating below 3.5, and that was 3.49; and only one of the 111 performance statements received a rating below 3.0, and that was 2.96. Of the 23 competencies, eight were considered "advanced," and the remaining 16 were considered as more generic skills. None of the competencies were seen as being demonstrated by novice designers only.

Application of These Findings

The current ibstpi competency team carefully reviewed the results of the 2000 ibstpi study. It was used as the foundation for the work on the revision. The competencies and performance statements from this study were examined, and revisions were undertaken based on new developments and directions in the field and based on the results of a recent survey undertaken with the alumni of a leading ID graduate program.

STUDY OF ALUMNI OF A LEADING ID GRADUATE PROGRAM

The purpose of this study was to examine the perceptions of practicing professionals as to the 2000 ibstpi ID competencies. The survey measured the frequency of use (with a 5-point scale of very often, often, sometimes, rarely, never) and the importance of the 23 competencies (essential, very important, somewhat important, of little importance, not at all important). In addition to the closed-ended ratings, respondents were asked two open-ended questions:

- What other competencies do you think instructional designers should possess?
- Please list one or more performance improvement competencies that you think should be added to the list of instructional design competencies

Results

A total of 133 respondents participated in the survey, with most possessing a master's or doctorate and working in academia; business and industry, or government; working as an instructional designer, performance improvement specialist, or training manager; having worked in the field for more than 6 years. The survey confirmed that all of the competencies were used sometimes to very often, and were somewhat important to essential. There were 65 open-ended responses, and they suggested the increasing importance of front-end assessment, performance and task analysis, cultural sensitivity, both instructional and noninstructional solutions, measurement and evaluation, involvement in strategic planning, systems thinking, management skills, and change management.

Application of These Findings

The current ibstpi competency team examined the survey results, particularly the open-ended responses. These open-ended responses suggested new or revised competencies and performance statements for use in drafting the set of competencies and performance statements for validation effort.

THE 2012 VALIDATION RESEARCH

This section provides the details on the competency development and validation process for the 2012 instructional designer competencies. We begin by describing the purpose and scope of the study and then turn to the specific procedures and instrumentation. This is followed by a description of the sample and the results of the validation.

PURPOSE AND SCOPE OF THE STUDY

The final set of instructional designer competencies and performance statements was based on a global validation effort. The validation work was focused on establishing:

- What the level of criticality was for each of the competencies and performance statements
- Whether the competencies and performance statements are considered essential or advanced
- Whether the competency and performance statement language was consistent with that used in the workplace
- Whether that language was culturally appropriate outside of North America
- Whether any critical areas of practice had been omitted

Ultimately, the aim of this research was to produce a final, validated set of competencies and performance statements for use in the profession.

PROCEDURES

In this section we present the three phases of the research study. These included a review of the foundational research, competency drafting, and competency validation and rewriting.

PHASE 1: IDENTIFICATION OF FOUNDATIONAL RESEARCH

An extensive review of programs, courses, and training modules in instructional design from universities and professional associations throughout the world provided the foundation for the present work. More specifically, the focus of this review was on changes in the instructional design field, in terms of new ID models, uses of technologies, and new approaches. In addition, a literature review examined some of the current research in the field.

As mentioned earlier, the survey of alumni of a leading graduate program gathered information from ID practitioners actively working in the field (e.g., academia, business and industry, government, etc.) helped to identify new behaviors, values, ethical concerns, and future visions in instruction design field. The areas of human performance, ID function management, and focus on technology integration competencies emerged that extended the 2000 standards.

PHASE 2: COMPETENCY DRAFTING

The base list of competencies reviewed and analyzed by a subset of the ibstpi directors who possessed particular expertise in different areas of instructional design and validation research instruments were reviewed and approved by the Institutional Review Board of Oregon State University. Based on the phase I research, additional competencies and performance statements were added to better articulate the competencies of instructional different levels of instructional designers. In addition, some competencies were restated and reorganized to clarify new roles of the instructional designer, suggesting career progression. A new classification level was also added based on the emerging role of the ID function manager and increased importance of managing ID functions and projects noted from the alumni study and new literature.

Six experts in instructional design from outside ibstpi also reviewed and commented on updated competencies and performance statements. The ibstpi team reviewed these comments and created an updated set of competencies for validation. This updated set was reviewed and approved by the ibstpi board of directors to be validated by the larger community of practice.

PHASE 3: COMPETENCY VALIDATION AND REWRITING

The final wording of domains, competencies, and performance statements were developed into a survey form for global validation. The instrument asked about the criticality of each competency and performance statement. The survey also included demographic items, and it included an open-ended item requesting suggestions for additions and modifications. It was then translated into Chinese, Japanese, Korean, and Spanish and then translated back into English. The translated versions were reviewed and approved by native speakers familiar with instructional design. In addition, all instruments and procedures were reviewed and approved by the Oregon State University Institutional Review Board. The five versions of the survey were administered through the use of an online survey system. The invitations to participate in the validation effort were sent through a variety of academic professionals, international associations and private lists in order to obtain responses from ID practitioners, researchers, and scholars around the world.

The results of the validation study were analyzed and reviewed by the subset of the ibstpi board, and a revised set of competencies and performance statements were developed. This revised set was reviewed by the full ibstpi board.

The revised set of competencies and performance statements was developed into a third survey, whose purpose was to identify the level of classification of each statement as: essential, advanced, or managerial. Again, the survey and procedures were approved by the Oregon State University Institutional Review Board. This survey was sent to 20 acknowledged experts in the ID field. The responses from 10 of these experts solidified the classification for each competency and performance statement.

INSTRUMENTATION

The instrument used in the criticality and validation study began with an introduction to the study, indicating its purpose and use and providing the informed consent materials approved by the Institutional Review Board of Oregon State University. Three separate sections in the survey included: the respondent demographic characteristics, the criticality statements, and additional, open-ended comments.

Respondent background characteristics. The section on background or demographic characteristics contained eight items. These items provided information needed to make generalizations of the results. The items included primary global regions for work, type of organization, highest level of education, degree in instructional design or closely related field, level of instructional design expertise, primary type of instruction delivered, primary audience for work, role (whether an employee or an external consultant), average years of instructional design work experience, and gender.

Criticality statements. The 22 competencies and 105 performance statements were listed, and respondents were asked to assign an importance rating to each in relation to their work as an instructional designer. The rating used a 5-point Liker-type scale where 1 represented "no importance" and 5 represented "high importance" to the respondent's work.

Competencies were shown in all capital letters and performance statements appeared sequentially numbered below. Table 6.1 shows the validation survey items for two performance statements related to the competencies *Communicate effectively in written, oral, and visual form.*

RESULTS

The following sections present the results from the online validation surveys. These results appear in three sections: (a) respondent background characteristics, (b) the criticality ratings, and relevant additional comments.

Respondent background characteristics. The ibstpi board sent out information to numerous professional associations for instructional designers around the world, academic programs in instructional design in several different countries, listservs, and professional networks, conference participants, and the worldwide contacts of ibstpi board members. Because the sample was not selected randomly, the profile data cannot be assumed to be truly representative of the practitioners for whom these standards have been developed. Nonetheless, there is considerable diversity among the respondents as described below.

Approximately 64% of the respondents came from the United States or Canada; 24% came from Asia, Australia, and New Zealand; 5% came from Europe; and the remaining 5% came from other parts of the world. Most instructional designers came from either educational institutions or from business and industry. Some 80% of instructional designers possessed a master's degree or higher, with 73% indicating that they had a degree in instructional design or a closely related field. Adding further corroboration to the profile, 86% of the respondents specified that they possessed an intermediate or expert level of expertise. Further, the average number of years of work experience in instructional design was 10.8 years. About 60% of the respondents indicated that they use a combination of instruction modes that include traditional (face to face), self study, and e-learning. Most of the design work is developed for higher education students (26%), middle managers (20%), or frontline production and/or service employees (17%). (See Table 6.2).

Criticality ratings. The following sections report the results of the ratings of criticality of the competencies and the performance statements. The discussion will begin with the general reactions. This will be followed by the competency rankings. The last section will present the details on the levels of expertise.

General reactions. Even though there were varied reactions to the revised set of competencies and performance statements, on the whole respondents gave the list a high level of support. High criticality ratings appeared

Table 6.1. An Example of the Items in the Validation Survey

PROFESSIONAL FOUNDATIONS: Use a scale of 1-5 to indicate how important this COMPETENCY 'Communicate effectively in visual, oral, and written form' and its ten PERFORMANCE STATEMENTS are in relation to your work as an instructional designer.

	1	2	3	4	5
	No Importance		Moderate Importance		High Importance
COMMUNICATE EFFECTIVELY IN VISUAL, ORAL, AND WRITTEN FORM					
a) Write and edit messages that are clear, concise, and grammatically correct					
b) Deliver presentations that effectively engage audiences and communicate clear messages					

Additional comments. The survey contained three open-ended items. These sought information on any competencies that should be added or reworded and asked for general feedback.

Table 6.2. Profile of the Instructional Designer Respondents

Characteristic	Respondents N	%
Primary Region of Work (*n* = 1001)		
U.S./Canada	641	64%
Asia, Australia, & New Zealand	259	26%
Europe	51	5%
Other	50	5%
Portion of Job with ID Focus (*n* = 955)		
20% or less	234	25%
21-40%	186	19%
41-60%	206	22%
61-80%	175	18%
81-100%	154	16%
Type of Organization (*n* = 958)		
Business/Industry	269	28%
Health Care	56	6%
Education	374	39%

K-12 Education Institution—77 (21%)

Higher Education Institution—297 (79%)

(Table continues on next page)

Table 6.2.   Continued

Characteristic	Respondents N	Respondents %
Govt./Military	109	11%
Other	150	16%
Highest Level of Education (n = 978)		
Seconday/High school or equivalent	11	1%
Undergraduate degree or equivalent	154	16%
Master's degree or equivalent	511	52%
Doctoral	267	27%
Other	35	4%
Degree in ID ($n = 972$)		
Yes	712	73%
No	260	27%
Level of ID Expertise ($n = 643$)		
Novice	90	14%
Intermediate	261	41%
Expert	292	45%
Type of Instruction ($n = 640$)		
Traditional (face-to-face)	81	13%
Self-Study	12	2%
e-Learning	161	25%
Combination of the Above	386	60%
Role ($n = 633$)		
Employee/Internal Consultant	475	75%
External Consultant	158	25%
Primary Audience (multiple sections allowed)**		
Executive	77	8%
Middle Managers	206	20%
Clerical Staff	30	3%
Front Line Production/Service Employees	170	17%
K-12 Students	92	9%
Higher Education Students	260	26%
General Public	63	6%
Other	116	11%
Gender ($n = 633$)		
Female	378	60%
Male	255	40%
Average Years of ID Work Experience ($n = 956$)		
10.82 Years for 956 respondents		

for most of the items, using a 5-point importance scale (5 indicated a very high rating, 3 was moderate, and 1 indicated that the item was not important at all.)

Table 6.3 presents the ratings for the five competency domains, showing the number and percentage of competencies within each domain receiving the various averages in ratings.

Table 6.4 displays the ratings for the performance statements within the five domains, again indicating the number and percentage of performance statements having certain levels of ratings. The results show that *professional foundations, planning and analysis,* and *design and development* are more highly rated than *evaluation and implementation* and *management.*

A further indication as to the level of general support for the competencies appeared in the responses to the open-ended items. Most of the respondents (78%) did not indicate any additional competencies in response to the question: "Are there any skills critical to being an instructional designer that are not included in this list? Please describe." The following are typical of the responses from those who made some comment:

- All have been addressed.
- None that I can think of at the moment.
- I thought this list was extremely thorough and complete!

Table 6.3. Criticality Ratings of Competencies Within Domains

| | Criticality Rating Range | | | | | | | |
| | 4.5-5.0 Very High− | | 4.0-4.49 High+ | | 3.5-3.99 High− | | Total Across Competency Domains | |
Competency Domain	N	%	N	%	N	%	N	%
Professional Foundations	0	0%	5	100%	0	0%	5	100%
Planning & Analysis	0	0%	4	100%	0	0%	4	100%
Design & Development	1	14%	4	57%	2	29%	7	100%
Evaluation & Implementation	0	0%	2	67%	1	33%	3	100%
Management	0	0%	2	67%	1	33%	3	100%
Total Across Competencies	1	5%	17	77%	4	18%	22	100%

Competency ratings. Table 6.5 provides more specific results on the domains and competencies. It shows the mean criticality rating and the related variance for each individual competency. The variances across the competencies appear to be similar, with a few exceptions. Specifically, the following competencies show slightly larger variances: *Apply business skills to managing the instructional design function*; *Plan noninstructional interventions*; and *Implement, disseminate, and diffuse instructional and noninstructional interventions*. Finally, Table 6.5 shows the rankings of the competencies, based on the mean criticality ratings; thus, the competencies are ranked from 1 (as the most critical) to 22 (as the least critical).

The top three ranked competencies were those within the *design and development* domain: *design learning assessment* (number 16), *design instructional interventions* (number 12), and *organize instructional design and/or products to be designed, developed, and evaluated* (number 11). The next ranked competency was within the *professional foundations* domain: *communicate effectively in visual, oral, and written form* (number 1). It should be noted that these results are somewhat different than those appearing in Richey, Fields, and Foxon (2001). In that earlier study, the highest ranked competency was *communicate effectively in visual, oral, and written form*. Furthermore the three highest ranked competencies in the present study received much lower rankings in the Richey, Fields, and Foxon study. That the three highest ranked competencies came from the design and development domain should not be surprising, however. These skills form the basis for the instructional design profession.

The lowest ranked competency was that of *plan noninstructional interventions* (number 13). Given that the instructional design field recognizes that on-the-job performance can be enhanced through more than instructional interventions, it is surprising that the competency received such a low rating (mean = 3.61). Also, it may be that the inclusion of "noninstructional" interventions resulted in a low rating for *implement, disseminate, and diffuse instructional and noninstructional interventions*. The final item receiving a low rating was that of *apply business skills to managing the instructional design function*. This lower rating may have resulted from the fact that many respondents were not in a managerial-type position.

Levels of expertise. Table 6.5 also presents summary results of the expertise ratings. Twelve of the competencies were considered essential. Another eight competencies were associated with experienced or expert designers (listed as "advanced" in the table). The remaining two competencies were viewed as managerial.

The instructional design field today is far more sophisticated and complex than in 1986 or in 2001. Design teams, rather than individuals, commonly complete projects; and there are an increasing number of design departments or design functions. Because of the complexity of the job,

**Table 6.5. Criticality Ratings of
the ibstpi Instructional Designer Competencies**

Competency	*N (Average)*	*Mean Criticality Rating (1-5; 5 High)*	*SD*	*Criticality Rank*	*Level of Expertise*
PROFESSIONAL FOUNDATIONS					
1. Communicate effectively in visual, oral, and written form.	777	4.33	0.83	4	Essential
2. Apply research and theory to the discipline of instructional design.	771	4.12	0.92	12	Advanced
3. Update and improve knowledge, skills, and attitudes pertaining to the instructional design process and related fields.	769	4.02	0.95	18	Essential
4. Apply data collection and analysis skills in instructional design projects.	771	4.09	0.93	14	Advanced
5. Identify and respond to ethical, legal, and political implications of design in the workplace.	769	4.22	0.94	8	Essential
PLANNING AND ANALYSIS					
6. Conduct a needs assessment in order to recommend appropriate design solutions and strategies.	707	4.23	0.91	7	Advanced
7. Identify and describe target population and environmental characteristics.	705	4.25	0.87	6	Essential
8. Select and use analysis techniques for determining instructional content.	702	4.26	0.84	5	Essential
9. Analyze the characteristics of existing and emerging technologies and their potential use.	704	4.09	0.89	13	Essential
DESIGN AND DEVELOPMENT					
10. Use an instructional design and development process appropriate for a given project.	653	4.14	0.95	11	Essential

(Table continues on next page)

Table 6.5.   Continued

Competency	N (Average)	Mean Criticality Rating (1-5; 5 High)	SD	Criticality Rank	Level of Expertise
DESIGN AND DEVELOPMENT					
11. Organize instructional programs and/or products to be designed, developed, and evaluated.	651	4.34	0.82	3	Essential
12. Design instructional interventions.	651	4.38	0.82	2	Essential
13. Plan noninstructional interventions.	646	3.61	1.21	22	Advanced
14. Select or modify existing instructional materials.	649.	3.98	0.99	19	Essential
15. Develop instructional materials.	651	4.19	0.95	9	Essential
16. Design learning assessment.	653	4.51	0.79	1	Advanced
EVALUATION & IMPLEMENTATION					
17. Evaluate instructional and noninstructional interventions.	634	4.02	1.03	17	Advanced
18. Revise instructional and noninstructional solutions based on data.	631	4.08	0.98	15	Essential
19. Implement, disseminate, and diffuse instructional and noninstructional interventions.	628	3.82	1.11	20	Advanced
MANAGEMENT					
20. Apply business skills to managing the instructional design function.	619	3.77	1.23	21	Managerial
21. Manage partnerships and collaborative relationships.	620	4.05	1.06	16	Managerial
22. Plan and manage instructional design projects.	620	4.15	1.02	10	Advanced

few designers are fully competent in all aspects of the profession. Tables 6.6 and 6.7 provide classifications as to the levels of expertise needed within the five domains.

There are patterns common to competencies found in Table 6.6. These include the following:

- 55% of the competencies are essential to the work of all designers.
- The competencies within the *Professional Foundations* domain are apparently not basic for all designers. There are advanced or expert skills as well as the general foundations.
- The essential competencies for all designers seem to be clustered in the *Design & Development* domain.
- The core set of advanced instructional design competencies appears to be primarily clustered in the *Professional Foundations* and the *Design & Development* domains.
- The core set of managerial competencies appear in the *Management* domain.

An examination of the levels of expertise of the performance statement shows a somewhat different pattern of results. These include:

- There is a somewhat more balanced distribution of performance statements across the expertise continuum of essential and advanced, particularly for the domains of *professional foundations, planning & analysis, design & development,* and *evaluation*.
- The essential competencies appear to be clustered in *professional foundations, planning & analysis,* and *design & development*.
- Managerial and advanced designers are the only ones with relevant performance statements in the *Management* domain.

Other patterns found with respect to performance statements in Table 6.7.

IMPLICATIONS FOR THE FINAL ID COMPETENCIES

By and large, the validation research confirmed the ID competencies and performance statements. There was, however, valuable input from the respondents that did result in minor changes to the listing. Most of these were simply wording changes that clarified the statements or emphasized aspects of the skill. Thus, the ibstpi instructional designer competencies provide the basis for improving the work instructional designers at all levels of expertise.

Table 6.6. An Overview of Competencies by Domains and Level of Expertise

Frequency by Competency Domain

Level of Expertise	Mean Competency Criticality Rank	Professional Foundations		Planning & Analysis		Design & Development		Evaluation & Implementation		Management		Total by Level of Expertise	
		N	%	N	%	N	%	N	%	N	%	N	%
Essential	4.22	3	60%	3	75%	5	71%	1	33%	0	0%	12	55%
Advanced	4.07	2	40%	1	25%	2	29%	2	67%	1	33%	8	36%
Managerial	3.87	0	0%	0	0%	0	0%	0	0%	2	67%	2	9%
TOTAL	4.13	5	100%	4	100%	7	100%	3	100%	3	100%	22	100%

Table 6.7. An Overview of Performance Statements by Domain and Level of Expertise

Frequency by Competency Domain

Level of Expertise	Professional Foundations		Planning & Analysis		Design & Development		Evaluation & Implementation		Management		Total by Level of Expertise	
	N	%	N	%	N	%	N	%	N	%	N	%
Essential	13	46%	10	50%	17	65%	4	29%	0	0%	44	42%
Advanced	15	54%	10	50%	9	35%	6	43%	4	24%	44	42%
Managerial	0	0%	0	0%	0	0%	4	29%	13	76%	17	16%
TOTAL	28	100%	20	100%	26	100%	14	100%	17	100%	105	100%

In summary, the validation research was an integral part of the competency validation process. The final list of instructional designer competencies and performance statements was based on the results of the validation research, which included an examination of the broader foundation of the empirical work described in the earlier chapters. The validation effort helped to confirm that the ibstpi instructional designer competency model was indeed applicable to instructional designers working in a variety of organizational settings and national and organizational cultures.

EPILOGUE

The new 2012 ibstpi instructional designer competencies are being presented in a far different time than those introduced in 2000 and 1986. Today, many practitioners, educators, managers of educational and design functions are working in environments bombarded with new digital technologies and new learning ideas that influence the design of instruction and development of learning environments. There are many solutions being developed that fail to support or facilitate content learning, rather that distract learners from content in favor of graphics, animations, games, social interactions, and other interactive features. The new ID competencies maintain a strong focus on design sciences and practices and the development of those competencies that suggest that designers can take advantage of the features of digital technologies and environments in ways that enhance learning. This focus on design is maintained in all instructional resources and learning environments whether paper-, classroom-, e-learning-, or blended-environment-based. The world is not completely ready for full online or e-learning. There are still many circumstances around the world where best practices in instruction and learning occur in traditional settings (e.g., classrooms, boardrooms, books and correspondences courses, television) or are offered with simple paper-based help- and job-aids. However, where technologies make sense, there are also examples of best practices in technology uses, either as enhancements to teaching or as integrated directly into learning. It is the application of instructional design competencies that make a difference in poor versus effective uses of technology resources—and the 2012 ibstpi instructional designer competency set remains focused on needs analysis, design, development, implementation, evaluation, and project management skills, knowledge, and attitudes, for all instructional and learning tools and environments.

The main differences between the 2012 instructional designers competencies and the 2000 instructional design competencies include:

- A wider range of levels of design expertise, that is, introduction of the managerial level
- References to other sets of specialty competency sets (e.g., evaluator, training manager)
- Emphasis on instructional design application in a world of rapidly emerging technologies
- Reflection in the changes of design practice, design theory, media design techniques, communication strategy enhancements, and cultural practices

As stated about the 2000 instructional design competencies, it would be naïve to presume that the 2012 instructional designer competencies would be any more stable than the 1986 version. It can be assumed that future designers may see these competencies as simplistic and dated as many now view the 2000 set of competencies. This 2012 set may also be seen as missing the mark in terms of technology skills given the explosion of new software, internet resources, applications, and technologies that have emerged in just the last few years. However, the focus of this set, as previous sets, remains firmly in the design sciences and practices.

It is difficult to project the nature of future changes in our field, other than anticipating a continuation of current trends. Technology will undoubtedly continue to advance, work settings will probably become even more complex, learning time may continue to be reduced to focus on productivity, and the term globalization may fade as international and cultural focuses become routine or common practice in all instructional design whether for schools, higher education, or business. Other societal changes—changes more difficult to predict—will likely also take place that will impact our field as they impact other disciplines. Future sets of the ibstpi instructional designer competencies will likely reflect these changes.

There remains a larger, yet partially answered question, as to the extent to which the field needs competencies for more specialized roles in the instructional design field. Based on data collected during global validation studies and reviews of current literature ibstpi has developed, validated, and published a set of program evaluators competencies (2008), is currently updating its set of competencies for training managers (2003), and is beginning to review its set of instructor competencies (2004). More uniquely, ibstpi is now also publishing a set of online learners competencies (2012). The questions continue to be raised as to whether more specific sets of competencies for training, performance, and instruction professionals are required. These questions are being explored by ibstpi. To a great extent, the answers will come from the global marketplace.

APPENDIXES

APPENDIX A:
IBSTPI INSTRUCTIONAL DESIGN COMPETENCIES (2000)

Professional Foundations

1. Communicate effectively in visual, oral and written form (essential).

   (a) Create messages that accommodate learner needs and characteristics, content and objectives (essential).
   (b) Write and edit text to produce messages that are clear, concise and grammatically correct (essential).
   (c) Apply principles of message design to page layout and screen design (essential).
   (d) Create or select visuals that instruct, orient or motivate (essential).
   (e) Deliver presentations that effectively engage and communicate (essential).
   (f) Use active listening skills in all situations (essential).
   (g) Present and receive information in a manner that is appropriate for the norms and tasks of the group or team (essential).
   (h) Seek and share information and ideas among individuals with diverse backgrounds and roles (essential).
   (i) Facilitate meetings effectively (essential).

2. Apply current research and theory to the practice of instructional design (advanced).

   (a) Promote, apply and disseminate the results of instructional design theory and research (advanced).
   (b) Read instructional design research, theory and practice literature (essential).
   (c) Apply concepts, techniques and theory of other disciplines to problems of learning, instruction and instructional design (advanced).

3. Update and improve one's knowledge, skills and attitude pertaining to instructional design and related fields (essential).

   (a) Apply developments in instructional design and related fields (advanced).
   (b) Acquire and apply new technology skills to instructional design practice (essential).
   (c) Participate in professional activities (essential).
   (d) Document one's work as a foundation for future efforts, publications or professional presentation (advanced).
   (e) Establish and maintain contacts with other professionals (essential).

4. Apply fundamental research skills to instructional design projects (advanced).

   (a) Use a variety of data collection tools and procedures (advanced).
   (b) Apply appropriate research and methodologies to needs assessment and evaluation (advanced).
   (c) Use basic statistical techniques in needs assessment and evaluation (advanced).
   (d) Write research and evaluation reports (advanced).

5. Identify and resolve ethical and legal implications of design in the work place (advanced).

   (a) Identify ethical and legal dimensions of instructional design practice (advanced).
   (b) Anticipate and respond to ethical consequences of design decisions (advanced).
   (c) Recognize and respect intellectual property rights of others (essential).

(d) Recognize the ethical and legal implications and conse-quences of instructional products (advanced).

(e) Adhere to regulatory guidelines and organization policies (essential).

Planning and Analysis

6. Conduct a needs assessment (essential).

   (a) Describe the problem and its dimensions, identifying the discrepancies between current and desired performance (essential).

   (b) Clarify the varying perceptions of needs and their implica-tions (advanced).

   (c) Select and use appropriate needs assessment tools and tech-niques (essential).

   (d) Determine the possible causes of the problem and potential solutions (essential).

   (e) Recommend and advocate noninstructional solutions when appropriate (advanced).

   (f) Complete a cost benefit analysis for recommended solutions (advanced).

7. Design a curriculum or program (essential).

   (a) Determine the scope of the curriculum or program (essential).

   (b) Specify courses based upon needs assessment outcomes (essential).

   (c) Sequence courses for learners and groups of learners (essential).

   (d) Analyze and modify existing curricula or program to insure adequate content coverage (essential).

   (e) Modify an existing curriculum or program to reflect changes in society, the knowledge base, technology or the organization (advanced).

8. Select and use a variety of techniques for determining instructional content (essential).

   (a) Identify content requirements in accordance with needs assessment findings (essential).

   (b) Elicit, synthesize and validate content from subject matter experts and other resources (advanced).

(c) Determine the breadth and depth of intended content coverage given instructional constraints (advanced).

(d) Determine prerequisites given the type of subject matter, the needs of the learners and the organization (essential).

(e) Use appropriate techniques to analyze varying types of content (essential).

9. Identify and describe target population characteristics (essential).

(a) Determine characteristics of the target population influencing learning and transfer (essential).

(b) Analyze, evaluate and select learner profile data for use in a particular design situation (advanced).

10. Analyze the characteristics of the environment (essential).

(a) Identify aspects of the physical and social environments that impact the delivery of instruction (essential).

(b) Identify environmental and cultural aspects that influence attitudes toward instructional interventions (advanced).

(c) Identify environmental and cultural factors that influence learning, attitudes and performance (advanced).

(d) Identify the nature and role of varying work environments in the teaching and learning processes (advanced).

(e) Determine the extent to which organizational mission, philosophy and values influence the design and success of a project (advanced).

11. Analyze the characteristics of existing and emerging technologies and their use in an instructional environments (essential).

(a) Specify the capabilities of existing and emerging technologies to enhance motivation, visualization, interaction, simulation and individualization (essential).

(b) Evaluate the capacity of a given infrastructure to support selected technologies (advanced).

(c) Assess the benefits of existing and emerging technologies (essential).

12. Reflect upon the elements of a situation before finalizing design solutions and strategies (essential).

(a) Generate multiple solutions to a given problem situation (advanced).

(b) Remain open to alternative solutions until sufficient data have been collected and verified (essential).

(c) Assess the consequences and implications of design decisions on the basis of prior experience, intuition, and knowledge (advanced).

(d) Revisit selected solutions continuously and adjust as necessary (advanced).

Design and Development

13. Select, modify or create a design and development model appropriate for a given project (advanced).

    (a) Consider multiple design and development models (advanced).
    (b) Select or create a model suitable for the project based on an analysis of model elements (advanced).
    (c) Modify the model if project parameters change (advanced).
    (d) Provide a rationale for the selected design and development model (advanced).

14. Select and use a variety of techniques to define and sequence the instructional content and strategies (essential).

    (a) Use appropriate techniques to identify the conditions that determine the scope of the instructional content (essential).
    (b) Use appropriate techniques to specify and sequence instructional goals and objectives (essential).
    (c) Select appropriate media and delivery systems (essential).
    (d) Analyze the learning outcomes and select appropriate strategies (essential).
    (e) Analyze the instructional context and select appropriate strategies (essential).
    (f) Select appropriate participation and motivational strategies (essential).
    (g) Select and sequence assessment techniques (essential).
    (h) Prepare a design document and circulate for review and approval (essential).

15. Select or modify existing instructional materials (essential).

    (a) Identify existing instructional materials for reuse or modification consistent with instructional specifications (essential).

(b) Select materials to support the content analyses, proposed technologies, delivery methods and instructional strategies (essential).

(c) Use cost-benefit analyses to decide whether to modify, purchase or develop instructional materials (advanced).

(d) Work with subject matter experts to validate material selection or modification (essential).

(e) Integrate existing instructional materials into the design (essential).

16. Develop instructional materials (essential).

(a) Develop materials that support the content analyses, proposed technologies, delivery methods and instructional strategies (essential).

(b) Work with subject matter experts during the development process (essential).

(c) Produce instructional materials in a variety of delivery formats (essential).

17. Design instruction that reflects an understanding of the diversity of learners and groups of learners (essential).

(a) Design instruction that accommodates different learning styles (essential).

(b) Be sensitive to the cultural impact of instructional materials (essential).

(c) Accommodate cultural factors that may influence learning in the design (essential).

18. Evaluate and assess instruction and its impact (essential).

(a) Construct reliable and valid test items using a variety of formats (advanced).

(b) Identify the processes and outcomes to be measures given the identified problem and proposed solutions (essential).

(c) Develop and implement formative evaluation plans (essential).

(d) d Develop and implement summative evaluation plans (essential).

(e) Develop and implement confirmative evaluation plans (advanced).

(f) Determine the impact of instruction on the organization (advanced).

(g) Identify and assess the sources of evaluation data (essential).

(h) Manage the evaluation process (advanced).

(i) Discuss and interpret evaluation reports with stakeholders (advanced).

Implementation and Management

19. Plan and manage instructional design projects (advanced).

   (a) Establish project scope and goals (advanced).
   (b) Use a variety of techniques and tools to develop a project plan (advanced).
   (c) Write project proposals (advanced).
   (d) Develop project information systems (advanced).
   (e) Monitor multiple instructional design projects (advanced).
   (f) Allocate resources to support the project plan (advanced).
   (g) Select and manage internal and external consultants (advanced).
   (h) Monitor congruence between performance and project plans (advanced).
   (i) Troubleshoot project problems (advanced).
   (j) Debrief design team to establish lessons learned (advanced).

20. Promote collaboration, partnerships and relationships among the participants in a design project (advanced).

   (a) Identify how and when collaboration and partnerships should be promoted (advanced).
   (b) Identify stakeholders and the nature of their involvement (advanced)
   (c) Identify subject matter experts to participate in the design and development process (advanced).
   (d) Build and promote effective relationships that may impact a design project (advanced).
   (e) Determine how to use cross functional teams (advanced).
   (f) Promote and manage the interactions among team members (advanced).
   (g) Plan for the diffusion of instructional or performance improvement products (advanced).

21. Apply business skills to managing instructional design (advanced).

   (a) Link design efforts to strategic plans of the organization (advanced).

    (b) Establish strategic and tactical goals for the design function (advanced).

    (c) Use a variety of techniques to establish standards of excellence (advanced).

    (d) Develop a business case to promote the critical role of the design function (advanced).

    (e) Recruit, retain and develop instructional design personnel (advanced).

    (f) Provide financial plans and controls for the instructional design function (advanced).

    (g) Maintain management and stakeholder support of the design function (advanced).

    (h) Market services and manage customer relations (advanced).

22. Design instructional management systems (advanced).

    (a) Establish systems for documenting learner progress and course completion (advanced).

    (b) Establish systems for maintaining records and issuing reports of individual and group progress (advanced).

    (c) Establish systems for diagnosing individual needs and prescribing instructional alternatives (advanced).

23. Provide for the effective implementation of instructional products and programs (essential).

    (a) Use evaluation data as a guide for revision of products and programs (advanced).

    (b) Update instructional products and programs as required (essential).

    (c) Monitor and revise the instructional delivery process as required (essential).

    (d) Revise instructional products and programs to reflect changes in professional practice or policy (essential).

    (e) Revise instructional products and programs to reflect changes in the organization or the target population (essential).

    (f) Recommend plans for organizational support of instructional programs (advanced).

24. Apply the learning and instructional theory (essential).

    (a) Compare and contrast critical attributes of learning and instructional theory (essential).

    (b) Develop principles from each theory (advanced).

(c) Apply each theory to the design of instructional materials (advanced).

(d) Justify the use of a particular theory in a given situation (advanced).

APPENDIX B:
GLOSSARY OF IBSTPI INSTRUCTIONAL DESIGN TERMS

Advanced capabilities—those knowledge, skills, and judgments demonstrated by experienced and expert designers. Applied to both competencies and performance statements.

Assessment—a measure of individual learning for various purposes, including a determination of readiness for learning, monitoring progress, and measuring achievement after instruction.

Benchmarking—the process of comparing curricula and other organizational information with best practice program.

Business case—the business-related reason for which a training or performance intervention is needed.

Consultant—an individual or organization retained to work on a project because of specific expertise. May be internal to one's organization or external. Related term: Contractor.

Competency—a knowledge, skill or attitude that enables one to effectively perform the activities of a given occupation or function to the standards expert in employment. Related term: Competence.

Confirmative evaluation—the process of determining whether over time learners have maintained their level of competence, the instructional materials remain effective, and the organizational problems have been solved. Confirmative evaluation occurs after formative and summative evaluation (Seels & Richey, 1994, p.126).

Cost benefit analysis—a comparison of the economic benefits of the program to the actual and opportunity costs of the program. Related term: Trade-off analysis.

Criticality—he extent to which a behavior or activity is viewed as essential to a designer's job.

Cross-functional teams—teams in which instructional designers work with specialists from other fields, such as organizational development, and multi-media development and engineering.

Curriculum—a large body of organized and sequential instruction, consisting of programs and courses. May also refer to the aggregate of modules or courses directed toward a common goal of a given organization, or a collection of required readings.

Customer—a person or organization for which a service is performed. May be internal to one's organization or external. Related term: Client.

Delivery system—a means of organizing, presenting, or distributing instruction, typically employing a variety of media, methods and materials.

Domain—a cluster of related competencies. Other uses: a subject matter area.

E-learning technologies—a person with expertise in delivery of content via all electronic media, audio/video taped, interactive TV, and CD-ROM.

Emerging technologies—new techniques, tools and equipment used in designing or delivering instruction, including virtual reality, electronic, performance support systems, and multi-user object-oriented domains.

Emerging technologies—new techniques, tools and equipment used in designing or delivering instruction, including virtual reality, electronic performance support systems, and multiuser object-oriented domains.

Essential Capabilities—those knowledge, skills, and judgments that all designers should be able to demonstrate. Applied to both competencies and performance statements.

Evaluation—the process of determining the adequacy, value, outcomes and impact of instruction and learning (adapted from Seels & Richey, 1994, p.128).

Expert instructional designer—a person with a foundation of formal training in the field, typically a graduate degree, substantial work experience, and the facility to anticipate design problems and quickly identify effective design solutions. Related term: Experienced instructional designer.

Expertise—the level of knowledge and experience demonstrated by designers who are typically categorized as either novice, experienced, or expert.

Formative evaluation—gathering information on the adequacy of an instructional product or program and using this information as a basis for further development (Seels & Richey, 1994, p.128)

Fundamental research skills—those skills which are basic to scientific investigation, including the design of exploratory studies and field tests, instrument design and data collection techniques, and the interpretation and analysis of qualitative and quantitative data.

Individualization—tailoring instruction to meet the abilities, knowledge, skills, interests, motivation and goals of individual learners.

Instruction—a planned process that facilitates learning.

Instructional context—the physical and psychological environment in which instruction is delivered or which transfer occurs. Related term: Learning environment.

Instructional design—systematic instructional planning including needs assessment, development, evaluation, implementation and maintenance of materials and programs. Related term: Instructional systems design.

Instructional design theory—a set of scientific principles relating to instructional methods, learner characteristics, learning environments, and outcomes. Typically derived from or tested by empirical research.

Instructional goal—a general statement of learner outcomes, related to an identified problem and needs assessment, and achievable through instruction (Dick & Carey, 1996, p.23).

Instructional objective—a detailed description of what learners will be able to do having completed a unit of instruction (Dick & Carey, 1996, p. 119). Related Terms: Learning outcome, behavioral objective, performance objective.

Instructional products—content-related items such as books, job aids, student and instructor guides, and web pages.

Instructional strategy—a general approach to selecting and sequencing learning activities. Related Term: Teach methods.

Instructional Systems Design—an organized procedure for developing instructional materials, programs, or curricula; includes the steps of analyzing, designing, developing, implementing, and evaluating. Related Term: Instructional design, instructional systems development.

Intellectual property—the technological or process knowledge and capabilities that an organization or an individual has developed. Typically protected by copyright.

Learner profile data—descriptions of the learner characteristics pertinent to instruction, including factors such as age, skill level, education and work experience. Related Term: Target population characteristics.

Learning—a relatively stable change knowledge or behavior as a result of experience.

Learning style—an individual's preferred means of acquiring knowledge and skills. Related Term: Cognitive style, multiple intelligence.

Media—the means by which instruction is presented to the learner. Typically classified in terms of the perceptual channels employed, such as visual or auditory media.

Message—a meaningful unit that may take alternative forms, including written, visual or oral. Messages may be instructional, informational, or motivational.

Multi-media—the integration of various forms of media for instructional purposes. Typically involving computer graphics, animation, video, sound, and text.

Needs assessment—a systematic process for determining goals, identifying discrepancies between optimal and actual performance, and establishing priorities for action (Briggs, 1977, p. xxiv). Related Term: Training needs assessment, needs analysis, front-end analysis, task and subject matter analysis.

Novice instructional designer—a person who has received basic training and education in instructional design fundamentals, but has little or no actual on-the-job work experience.

Organizational mission—a description of the organization's purpose, values, strategic position and long term care goals.

Organizational philosophy—a description of an organization's values and beliefs with regard to ho it tends to act and interact with its environment.

Organizational values—a stable set of long term aspirations and actions that the organization uses to make strategic choices. Related Term: Corporate culture.

Performance improvement—the process of designing or selecting interventions directed toward a change in behavior, typically on the job. Related Terms: performance technology, human performance technology.

Performance statement—a detailed explanation of activities comprising a competency statement.

Professional activities—conduct which enhances the skill and knowledge of the instructional design practitioner, including attending professional association meetings and conferences, reading relevant texts, or networking with other practitioners.

Program—a unit of instruction consisting of two or more courses, modules, workshops, seminars and the like.

Project information system—organized processes and database used to manage projects and resources.

Reliability—the degree to which items consistently yield the same or comparable results.

Stakeholder—people with vested interest in project outcomes.

Strategic Plan—a process for allocating resource to achieve long-range organizational goals.

Subject matter expert—a content specialist who advises or assists the designer. Related Terms: SME, content expert.

Summative evaluation—systematically gathering information on the adequacy and outcomes of an instructional intervention and using this information to make decisions about utilization (Seels & Richey, 1994. p. 134).

Tactical goals—statements that specify short-term actions required to achieve an organizations strategic goals.

Target population—those persons for whom an instructional intervention in intended. Related Terms: The learners, the learner group.

Transfer—the application of knowledge and skills acquired in training to another environment, typically a work setting.

Validation—the process of determining the extent to which competencies and performance statements are supported by profession.

Validity—the degree to which measures what they are intended to measure. Related Terms: Valid test items.

Visuals—graphics or teaching materials that pictorially describe ideas or convey meanings, including overhead transparencies, screen graphics or icons. Related Terms: Visual aids.

APPENDIX C: IBSTPI CODE OF ETHICAL STANDARDS FOR INSTRUCTIONAL DESIGNERS

1. Guiding Standards: Responsibilities to others

    (a) Provide efficient, effective, workable, and cost effective solutions to client problems.
    (b) Systematically improve human performance to accomplish valid and appropriate individual goals.
    (c) Facilitate individuals.
    (d) Help clients make informed decisions.
    (e) Inform others of potential ethical violations and conflicts of interest.
    (f) Educate clients in matters of instructional design and performance improvement.

2. Guiding Standards: Social Mandates

    (a) Support humane, socially responsible goals and activities for individuals and organizations.
    (b) Make professional decisions based upon moral and ethical positions regarding societal issues.
    (c) Consider the impact of planned interventions upon individuals, organizations, and the society as a whole.

3. Guiding Standards: Respecting the Rights of Others

    (a) Protect the privacy, candor and confidentiality of client and colleague information and communication.
    (b) Show respect for copyright and intellectual property.
    (c) Do not misuse client or colleague information for personal gain.

(d) Do not represent the ideas or work of others as one's own.
(e) Do not make false claims about others.
(f) Do not discriminate unfairly in actions related to hiring, retention, and advancement.

4. Guiding Standards: Professional Practice

(a) Be honest and fair in all facets of one's work.
(b) Share skills and knowledge with other professionals.
(c) Acknowledge the contributions.
(d) Aid and be supportive of colleagues.
(e) Commit time and effort to the development of the profession.
(f) Withdraw from clients who do not act ethically or when there is a conflict or interest.

REFERENCES

American Educational Research Association, American Psychological Association, and National Council on Measurement in Education. (1999). *Standards for educational and psychological testing.* Washington, DC: American Educational Research Association.

American Society for Training and Development. (2011). *ASTD State of the Industry Report (SOIR).* Retrieved from http://www.astd.org/content/research/stateOfIndustry.htm.

Anderson, V. (2009). Desperately seeking alignment: Reflections of senior line managers and HRD executives. *Human Resource Development International, 12*(3), 263-277. doi:10.1080/13678860902982009

Atchison, B. J. (1996). *Roles and competencies of instructional design as identified by expert instructional designers* (Unpublished doctoral dissertation). Wayne State University, Detroit, MI. Retrieved from: http://digitalcommons.wayne.edu/dissertations/AAI9628870/

Banathy, B. H. (1968). *Instructional systems.* Belmont, CA: Fearon.

Briggs, L. (1977). *Instructional Design: Principles and applications.* Englewood cliffs, NJ: Educational Technology Publications.

Brinkerhoff, R. O. (2003). *The success case method: Find out quickly what's working and what's not.* San Francisco, CA: Berrett-Koehler.

Brinkerhoff, R. O. (2005a). Success case method. In S. Mathison (Ed.), *Encyclopedia of evaluation.* Thousand Oaks, CA: SAGE.

Brinkerhoff, R. O. (2005b). The success case method: A strategic evaluation approach to increasing the value and effect of training. *Advances in Developing Human Resources, 7*(1), 86-101.

Brinkerhoff, R. O. (2006). *Telling training's story: Evaluation made simple, credible, and effective.* San Francisco, CA: Berrett-Koehler.

Carr-Chellman, A. A. (2006). *User-design.* Mahwah, NJ: Lawrence Erlbaum Associates.

Carr-Chellman, A. A., Cuyar, C., & Breman, J. (1998). User-Design: A Case Application in Health Care Training. *Educational Technology Research and Development, 46*(4), 97-114.

151

Catano, V. (1998). Appendix 1: Competencies: A review of the literature and bibliography, Canadian council of Human Resources Associations. Retrieved from http://www.chrpcanda.com/en/phaslreport/appendix.asp

Chen, E. H. (2004). A review of learning theories from visual literacy. *Journal of Educational Computing, Design & Online Learning, 5*(3). Retrieved from http://coe.ksu.edu/jecdol/Vol_5/html/VisualLiteracy.htm

Cousins, J. B., & Earl, L. E. (1992). The case for participatory evaluation. *Educational Evaluation and Policy Analysis, 14*(4), 397-418.

Cousins, J. B., & Earl, L. E. (1995). *Participatory evaluation in education.* London, England: Falmer Press.

Cousins, J. B., & Whitmore, E. (1998). Framing participatory evaluation. *New Directions for Evaluation, 80,* 5-23.

Cristensen, T. K., & Osguthorpe, R. T. (2004). How do instructional design practitioners make instructional strategy decisions? *Performance Improvement Quarterly, 17*(3), 45-65.

DeVos, A., DeHauw, S., & Van der Heijden, B. (2011). Competency development and career success: The mediating role of employability. *Journal of Vocational Behavior, 79,* 438-447.

Dick, D. (1987). A history of instructional design and its impact on educational psychology. In J. A. Glover & R. R. Ronning (Eds.), *Historical foundations of educational psychology* (pp. 183-202). New York, NY: Plenum Press.

Dick, W., & Carey, L. (1978). *The systematic design of instruction.* Glenview, IL: Scott, Foresman and Company.

Dick, W, Carey, & L. & Carey, J. (1996). *The systematic design of instruction* (4th ed.). New York, NY: HarperCollins.

Dick, W, Carey, L., & Carey, J. (2005). *The systematic design of instruction* (6th ed.). Boston, MA: Allyn & Bacon.

Dick, W., Watson, K., & Kaufman, R. (1981). Deriving competencies: Consensus versus model building. *Educational Researcher, 10*(10) 5-10.

Ellaway, R., & Master, K. (2008). AMEE Guide 52: e-learning in medical education Part I: Learning, teaching and assessment. *Medical Teacher, 30,* 455-473.

Ertmer, P. A., York, C. S., & Gedik, N. (2009). Learning from the pros: How experienced designers translate instructional design models into practice. *Educational Technology, 49*(1), 19-26.

Eseryel, D. (2006). Expert conceptualizations of the domain of instructional design: An investigative study on the deep assessment methodology for complex problem-solving outcomes. *Dissertation Abstracts International, 67*(11). (UMI No. 3241853).

Flanagan, J. (1949). A new approach to evaluating personnel: Critical incidents. *Personnel, 26,* 35-42.

Flanagan, J. (1954). The critical incident technique. *Psychological Bulletin, 51*(4), 327-358.

Foxon, M., Roberts, R., & Spannaus, T. (2003). *Training manager competencies: The standards* (3rd ed.). Syracuse, NY: ERIC Clearinghouse on Information & Technology.

Friedlander, P. (1996). Competency-driven, component-based curriculum architecture. *Performance Improvement, 35*(2), 14-21.

Fugate, M., & Kinicki, A. J. (2008). A dispositional approach to employability: Development of a measure and test of implications for employee reactions to organizational change. *Journal of Occupational & Organizational Psychology, 81*(3), 503-527.

Fugate, M., Kinicki, A. J., & Ashforth, B. E. (2004). Employability: A psycho-social construct, its dimensions, and applications. *Journal of Vocational Behavior, 65,* 14-38.

Gagne, R. M. (1965). *The conditions of learning* (1st ed.). New York, NY: Holt, Rinehart & Winston.

Glaser, R. (1965). Toward a behavioral science base for instructional design. In R. Glaser (Ed.), *Teaching machines and programmed learning, II: Data and directions.* Washington, DC: National Education Association.

Gogus, A., Koszalka, T., & Spector, J. M. (2009). Assessing conceptual representations of ill-defined problems. *Technology, Instruction, Cognition and Learning, 7*(1), 1-20.

Grabowski, B. L., & Small, R. V. (1997). Information, instruction, and learning: A hypermedia perspective. *Performance Improvement Quarterly,* 10 Year Anniversary Issue, *10*(1), 156-166.

Gustafson, K. L., & Branch, R. M. (1997). *Survey of instructional development models* (3rd ed.). Syracuse, NY: ERIC Clearinghouse on Information & Technology.

Gustafson, K. L., & Branch, R. M. (2002). *Survey of instructional development models* (4th ed.). Syracuse, NY: ERIC.

Harden, R. M., Gessner, L. H., Gunn. M., Issenberg, S. B., Pringle, S. D., & Stewart, A. (2011). Creating an e-learning module from learning objects using a commentary or "personal learning assistant." *Medical Teacher, 33,* 286-290.

Hardré, P. L., Ge, X., & Thomas, M. K. (2006). An investigation of development toward instructional design expertise. *Performance Improvement Quarterly, 19*(4), 63-90.

HR Guide to the Internet. (2012). Retrieved from http://www.hr-guide.com/

Industry Report. (1990). *Training, 27*(10), 31-76.

Industry Report. (1999). *Training, 36*(10), 37-80.

Jacobson, M. J. (2008). A design framework for educational hypermedia systems: Theory, research, and learning emerging scientific conceptual perspectives. *Educational Technology Research and Development, 56*(1), 5-28.

Jones, M. K., Li, Z., & Merrill, M. D. (1992). Rapid prototyping in automated instructional design. *Educational Technology Research and Development, 40*(4), 95-100.

Keller, J. M. (1983) Motivational design of instruction. In C .M. Reigeluth (Ed.), *Instructional design theories and models* (pp. 383-433). New York, NY: Lawrence Erlbaum Associates.

Keller, J. M. (1987). The systematic process of motivational design. *Performance & Instruction, 26*(9-10), 1-8.

Keller, J. M. (2010). *Design Learning and Performance: The ARCS model approach.* New York, NY: Springer.

Kierstead, J. (1998). Competencies and KSAO's, Research Directorate, Policy, Research and Communications Branch, Public Service Commission of Canada.

Kirkpatrick, D. L. (1959a, November). Techniques for evaluating programs. *Journal of the American Society of Training Directors (Training and Development Journal), 13*(11), 3-9.

Kirkpatrick, D. L. (1959b). Techniques for evaluating programs—Part 2: Learning. *Journal of the American Society of Training Directors (Training and Development Journal), 13*(12), 21-26.

Kirkpatrick, D. L. (1960a, January). Techniques for evaluating programs—Part 3: Behavior. *Journal of the American Society of Training Directors (Training and Development Journal), 14*(1), 13-18.

Kirkpatrick, D. L. (1960b, January). Techniques for evaluating programs—Part 4: Results." *Journal of the American Society of Training Directors (Training and Development Journal), 14*(1), 28-32.

Kirkpatrick, D. L. (1994). *Evaluating training programs: The four levels*. San Francisco, CA: Berrett-Koehler.

Klein, J. (1996). An analysis of content and survey of future direction. *Educational Technology Research & Development, 45*(3), 57-62.

Klein, J., Spector, M., Grabowski, B., & de la Teja (2004). *Instructor competencies: Standards for face-to-face, online, and blended settings*. Greenwich, CT: Information Age Publishing

Knox, I., & Wilmott, D. (2008) Virtual teams: worlds apart. Proceedings *ascilite* Melbourne 2008. 500-504. Retrieved from http://www.ascilite.org.au/conferences/melbourne08/procs/knox.pdf

Koschmann, T. (1996). *CSCL: Theory and practice of an emerging paradigm*. Mahwah, NJ: Lawrence Erlbaum Associates.

Koszalka, T., & Epling, J. (2010). A methodology for assessing elicitation of knowledge in complex domains: identifying conceptual representations of ill-structured problems in medical diagnostics. In D. Ifenthaler, P. Pirnay-Drummer, & N. M. (Eds.), *Computer-based diagnostics and systematic analysis of knowledge* (pp. 311-344). New York, NY: Springer.

Koszalka, T., & Ganesan, R., (2004). Designing online courses: A taxonomy to guide strategic us of features available in course management systems (CMS) in distance education. *Distance Education, 25*(2) 243-256.

Koszalka, T., & Ntloedibe-Kuswani, G. S. (2010). Literature on the safe and disruptive learning potential of mobile-technologies. *Distance Education, 31*(2), 139-150.

Koszalka, T., & Wu, Y. (2010). Instructional Design Issues in a Distributed Collaborative Engineering Design (CED) Instructional Environment. *Quarterly Review of Distance Education, 11*(2), 105-125.

Le Boterf, G. (2001). *Construire les compétences individuelles et collectives*. Paris, France: Éditions d'organisation.

LeMaistre, C. (1998). What is an expert instructional designer? Evidence of expert performance during formative evaluation. *Educational Technology Research & Development, 46*(3), 21-36.

Lucia, A. D., & Lepsinger, R. (1999). *The art and science of competency models: Pinpointing critical success factors in organization*. San Francisco, CA: Jossey-Bass/Pfeiffer.

Mager, R., & Pipe, P. (1984). *Analyzing performance problems, or you really oughta wanna* (2nd ed.). Belmont, CA: Lake Publishing.

Marrelli, A. F. (1998). An introduction to competency analysis and modeling. *Performance Improvement, 37*(5), 8-17.

Martin, F. (2008). Instructional design process and the importance of instructional alignment. White paper retrieved from http://www.florencemartin.net/site08/research/Martin_Instructional%20Design%20Process_Importance%20of%20Instructional%20Alignment_Aug08.pdf

McCelland, D. C. (1973). Testing for competence rather than for intelligence. *American Psychologist, 28*, 1-14.

McDonald, J., & Gibbons, A. (2009). Technology I, II, III: Criteria for understanding and improving the practice of instructional technology. *Educational Technology Research and Development, 57*(3), 377-392.

McLagan, P. A. (May 1997). Competencies: The next generation. *Training & Development,* 40-47.

Morrison, G., Ross, S., & Kemp, J. (2001). *Designing effective instruction* (3rd ed.). New York, NY: John Wiley & Sons.

Oliver, R. (1999). Exploring strategies for online teaching and learning. *Distance Education, 20*, 240-250.

Parry, S. B. (1998). Just what is a competency? (and why should you care?). *Training, 35*(6), 58-64.

Patton, M. Q. (2008). *Utilization-focused evaluation* (4th ed.). Thousand Oaks, CA: SAGE.

Perez, R. S., & Emery, C. D. (1995). Designer thinking: How novices and experts think about instructional design. *Performance Improvement Quarterly, 8*(3), 80-95.

Pettersson, R. (2007). Visual literacy in message design. *Journal of Visual Literacy, 27*(1), 61-90.

Pieters, J. M. (1997). Training for human resources development in industrial and professional organizations. In S. Dijkstra et al. (Eds.) *Instructional design: International perspectives. Volume 2: Solving instructional design problems* (pp. 315-340). Mahwah, NJ: Lawrence Erlbaum.

Reiser, R., & Dempsey, J. (2007). *Trends and issues in design and technology.* Upper Saddle River, NJ: Merrill Prentice-Hall.

Richey R., & Morrison, G. (2000). Instructional design in business and industry. In R. Reiser & J. Dempsey (Eds.), *Trends and issues in instructional technology.* New York, NY: Merrill.

Richey, R., & Morrison, G. R. (2000). Instructional design theory construction. In G. Anglin (Ed.), *Critical Issues in instructional technology,* Englewood, CO: Libraries Unlimited.

Richey, R. C. (1986). *The theoretical and conceptual basis of instructional design.* London, England: Kogan Page.

Richey, R. C., Fields, D. C., & Foxon, M. (2001). *Instructional design competencies: The standards* (3rd ed.). Syracuse, NY: ERIC Clearinghouse on Information & Technology.

Richey, R. C., Klein, J. D., & Tracey, M. W. (2011). *The instructional design knowledge base: Theory, research and practice.* New York, NY: Routledge.

Rogers, C. P., Graham, C. R., & Mayes, C. T. (2007). Cultural competence and instructional design: Exploration research into the delivery of online instruction cross-culturally. *Educational Technology Research and Development, 55*(2), 197-217.

Rosenberg, M., Coscarelli, W., & Hutchison, C. (1999). The origins and evolution of the field. In H. Stolovitch & E. Keeps (Eds.), *Handbook of Human Performance Technology* (2nd ed.). San Francisco, CA: Jossey-Bass/Pfeiffer.

Rothwell, W., & Kazanas, H. (1998). *Mastering the instructional design process* (2nd ed.). San Francisco, CA: Jossey-Bass.

Rowe, C. (1995). Clarifying the use of competence and competency models in recruitment, assessment and staff development. *Industrial and Commercial Training, 27*(11), 12.

Rowland, G. (1992). What do instructional designers actually do? An initial investigation of expert practice. *Performance Improvement Quarterly, 5*(2), 65-86.

Russ-Eft, D. F., Bober, M. J., de la Teja, I., Foxon, M., & Koszalka, T. A. (2008). *Evaluator competencies: The standards.* San Francisco, CA: Jossey-Bass.

Russ-Eft, D., & Preskill, H. (2009). *Evaluation in organizations: A systematic approach to enhancing learning, performance, and change* (2nd ed.). New York, NY: Basic Books.

Russ-Eft, D., & Preskill, H. (2005). In search of the holy grail: ROI evaluation in HRD. *Advances in Developing Human Resources, 7,* 71-85.

Seels, B. (1989). The instructional design movement in educational technology. *Educational Technology, 29*(5), 11-15.

Seels, B., & Glasgow, Z. (1997). *Making instructional design decisions.* Englewood Cliffs, NJ: Educational Technology Publications.

Seels, B. B., & Richey, R. C. (1994). *Instructional technology: The definition and domains of the field.* Bloomington, IN: Association for Educational Communications and Technology.

Silvern, L. (1971). *The evolution of systems thinking in education, 2nd edition.* Los Angeles, CA: Educational and Training Consultant.

Sims, R., & Koszalka, T. (2008). Competencies for the new-age instructional designer. In J. M. Spector, M. D. Merrill, J. J. G. van Merriënboer, & M. P. Driscoll (Eds.), *Handbook of Research on Educational Communications and Technology* (pp. 569-575). Mahwah, NJ: Lawrence Erlbaum Associates.

Sheehan, M. D., & Johnson, R. B. (2011). Philosophical and methodological beliefs of instructional design faculty and professionals. *Educational Technology Research and Development,* doi:10.1007/s11423-01109220-7

Smith, P., & Ragan, T. (2005). *Instructional design* (3rd ed.). Hoboken, NJ: Wiley & Sons.

Song, J. (1998). *An examination of the instructional design competencies written by the International Board of Standards for Training, Performance, and Instruction* (Unpublished master's thesis). St. Cloud, MN: St. Cloud State University.

Spector, J. M., Dennen, V. P., & Koszalka, T. (2006). Causal maps, mental models and assessing acquisition of expertise. *Technology, Instruction, Cognition and Learning, 3,* 167-183.

Spencer, L. M., & Spencer, S. M. (1993). *Competence at work: Models for superior performance.* New York, NY: John Wiley & Sons.

Stake, R. E. (1983). Responsive evaluation. In *International Encyclopedia of Education.* Oxford, England: Pergamon.

Staley, J., & Ice, P. (2009). *Instructional Design Project Management 2.0: A model of development and practice.* Paper presented at 25th annual conference on Distance Teaching and Learning. Retrieved from http://www.uwex.edu/disted/conference/Resource_library/proceedings/ 09_19400.pdf

Tanik, M. M., & Yeh, R. T. (1989). Rapid prototyping in software development. *Computer 22*(5), 9-10.

Taskforce on ID certification (1981). Competencies for the instructional/training development professional. *Journal of Instructional Development, 5*(1), 14-15.

Toolsema, B. (2003) *Werken met compententies. Naar een instrument voor de identificatie van competenties* [Working with competencies. A tool for the identification of competencies]. Doctoral dissertation, Twente University, Enschede, the Netherlands.

Torres, R., Preskill, H., & Piontek, M. (2004). *Evaluation strategies for communicating and reporting: Enhancing learning in organizations* (2nd ed.). Thousand Oaks, CA: SAGE.

Tripp, S. D., & Bichelmeyer, B. (1990). Rapid prototyping: An alternative instructional design strategy. *Educational Technology Research and Development, 38*(1), 31-44. doi:10.1007/BF02298246

Underwood, J., Hoadly, C., Lee, H., DiGiano, C., & Renniger, K. (2005). IDEA: Identifying design principles in educational applets. *Educational Technology Research and Development, 53*(2), 99-112.

Van der Heijde, C. M., & Van der Heijden, B. I. J. M. (2006). A competence-based and multidimensional operationalization and measurement of employability. *Human Resource Management, 45*(3), 449-476.

Van Merriënboer, J. J. G., Van der Klink, M. R., & Hendriks, M. (2002). *Competenties: Van complicaties tot compromis* [Competences: From complications to compromizes], Den Haag, The Netherlands: Onderwijsraad.

Van Merriënboer, J. J. G., & Martens, R. (2011). Computer-based tools for instructional design: An introduction to the special issue. *Educational Technology Research and Development, 59*(4), 5-9.

Visscher-Voerman, I. Gustafson, K., & Plomp, T. (1999). Educational design and development: An overview of paradigms. In J. van den Akker, R. M. Branch, K. Gustafson, N. Nieveen, & T. Plomp (Eds.), *Design approaches and tools in education and training* (pp. 15-28). Boston, MA: Kluwer Academic.

Wallington, C. J. (1981). Generic skills of an instructional designer. *Journal of Instructional Development, 4*(3) 28-32.

Wiley, D. (2002). *Instructional use of learning objects.* Agency for Instructional Technology and the Association for Educational Communications and Technology

Whitten, J. L., Bentley, L. D., & Barlow, V. M. (1989). *Systems analysis & design methods* (2nd ed.). Homewood, IL: Irwin.

Woodruff, C. (1991). Competent by any other name. *Personnel Management,* 38-43.

Wu, Y., & Koszalka, T. (2011). Instructional design of an Advanced Interactive Discovery Environment: Exploring team communication and technology use in collaborative engineering problem solving. In G. Vincenti & J. Braman (Eds.). *Multi-user virtual environments for the classroom: Practical approaches to teaching in virtual worlds*. Hershey, PA: IGI Global.

Young, J. I., & Van Mondfrans, A. P. (1972). Psychological implications of competency-based education. *Educational Technology, 12*(11), 15-18.

ABOUT THE AUTHORS

Tiffany A. Koszalka, PhD, is professor and chair of instructional design, development and evaluation at Syracuse University. Her research focus is the integration of learning, instruction, and technologies in instructional and learning environments. She has worked in a variety of corporate, K-12, and higher education environments designing, developing, implementing, and evaluating multimedia-based, distance, classroom, and blended instruction. She also helped establish international training centers in Europe and Asia. Dr. Koszalka is a former president of the design and development divisions for the Association for Educational Communications and Technology (AECT) and is a director for the International Board of Standards for Training, Performance, and Instruction (ibstpi). She collaborates with colleagues from universities, businesses, and government agencies around the world, has secured funding from NSF, NASA, NIH, and the Department of Education and publishes widely in the instructional sciences. Her most recent books are *Evaluator Competencies: Standards for the Practice of Evaluation in Organizations* (2008, Jossey-Bass) and *Regional Guidelines on Teacher Development for Pedagogy-Technology Integration* (2005, UNESCO).

Darlene Russ-Eft, PhD, is professor of adult education and higher education leadership in the College of Education at Oregon State University. Her most recent books are *Evaluation in Organizations: A Systematic Approach to Enhancing Learning, Performance, and Change* (2009, Basic Books), *Evaluator Competencies: Standards for the Practice of Evaluation in Organizations* (2008, Jossey-Bass), *A Practical Guide to Needs Assessment* (2007, Pfeiffer), and *Building Evaluation Capacity: 72 Activities for Teaching and Training* (2005, SAGE). Her recent research has included global studies to identify

159

and validate competencies of evaluators and of instructional designers. She is immediate past-president for the Academy of Human Resource Development (AHRD) and current director of the International Board of Standards for Training, Performance, and Instruction (ibstpi). She is a past editor of the *Human Resource Development Quarterly* and she received the 1996 Editor of the Year Award from Times Mirror, Outstanding Scholar Award from the AHRD, and Outstanding Research Article Award from ASTD.

Robert Reiser is associate dean for research, a university distinguished teaching professor and the Robert M. Morgan professor of instructional systems in the College of Education at Florida State University. He joined the Florida State faculty in 1976, after receiving his doctorate in educational technology from Arizona State University. Reiser has written over 75 journal articles and book chapters and 4 books in the field of instructional design and technology. His most recent book, *Trends and Issues in Instructional Design and Technology*, has received several book awards from major professional organizations in the field, including the Association for Educational Communications and Technology (AECT) and the International Society for Performance Improvement (ISPI). During the 37 years he has been at Florida State, Reiser has received several university awards, including a Developing Scholar Award, a Professorial Excellence Award, and the University Distinguished Teacher Award, the highest teaching award at Florida State.

Fernando A. Senior Canela, PhD, has over 30 years experience in the field of instructional design. This discipline he so passionately promotes, has allowed him to channel his curiosity and enthusiasm for the learning process though the design of customized learning solutions in corporate, nonprofit, and higher education environments in the United States, Mexico, Costa Rica, Puerto Rico, Chile and his native country of the Dominican Republic. Dr. Senior leads projects, develops teams, teachers in graduate programs, develops faculty, coaches organizations, and evaluates self-instructional, face-to-face, blended and online programs. He has contributed to projects funded by the National Science Foundation, the Inter-American Development Bank, and World Press Photo. As Learning Consultant at the Office of the Vice President for Academic Affairs at Universidad Andrés Bello in Santiago, Chile, he is currently supporting the institutional aspirations to obtain accreditation in the United States. He is the current president of the International Board of Standards for Training, Performance, and Instruction (ibstpi).

Barbara L. Grabowski (special guest-Forword), PhD, is a current ibstpi fellow, former president of the International Board of Standards for

Training, Performance, and Instruction (ibstpi), and professor emerita of instructional systems in the College of Education at Penn State University. Previously, she held academic appointments at the University of Maryland School of Medicine and Syracuse University. Between academic appointments, she designed, developed and evaluated a premier distance education program for nuclear reactor operators, and designed multimedia materials for industry, military, and medical environments at the University of Maryland University College. She has been internationally recognized for her design of innovative programs and has published widely, receiving two outstanding book awards from the Association for Educational Communications and Technology. She has been an invited keynote speaker on four continents. Her research focused on pedagogical uses of emerging technologies, with a special emphasis on online teaching and learning for K-12, college, and adult learners.

Clinton J. Wallington (special guest-Preface), PhD, is currently an adjunct professor in the Department of Hospitality and Service Management at the Rochester Institute of Technology (RIT). He has been chair of RIT's programs in audiovisual communications, instructional technology, and career and human resource development. Before his stint at RIT, he was research and communications director for the Association for Educational Communications and Technology (AECT) where he was responsible for all periodic and nonperiodic publications for 10 years. While at AECT he became involved in the original instructional design competencies effort and was even responsible for suggesting IBSTPI's name (terrible acronym, but politically sound). He spent two summers at Johnson Space Center as a NASA faculty fellow, where he survived NASA's high altitude/rapid decompression training and received an International Space Station program "Team Spirit Award." This led to teaching the first space tourism development course. Ironically Tiffany A. Koszalka and Fernando Senior-Canella are both graduates of the RIT Instructional Technology program. C. J. has a PhD from the University of Southern California, the home of "instructional technology."

64382657R10100

Made in the USA
Lexington, KY
06 June 2017